HCB
PUBLISHING

CONFIDENCE

HOW TO HAVE IT AND KEEP IT

CHRIS & KARENE LAMBERT-GORWYN AND
DAVID GIL CRISTOBAL

-in collaboration with-

**Jules Francis - Anna Goodwin - Emma Grace
Dr. Andrea Haas - Anni Jakenfelds - Molly Jones
Claudia R Knights - Mats Kolbjornsen
Christine Laidlaw - Mike Lawrence
Jane McDowell - Lisa Moore - Irma Prins
Simon Rogers - David Roylance - Sophie Thwaites**

CONFIDENCE – HOW TO HAVE IT AND KEEP IT –

ISBN: 978-1-8380061-8-1

Publisher

HCB Publishing Ltd.

London

United Kingdom

Printed in EU, UK, Canada and the United States of America

Table of Contents

DEDICATION 9

FOREWORD 11

INTRODUCTION 13

CONFIDENCE 15

Jules Francis *22*

What If I Told You That Food Cravings Are Your Body's Way Of Communicating? 23

Anna Goodwin *28*

Do You Feel Confident In Sales? 29

Emma Grace *34*

How To Fly When Your Wings Are Broken 37

Dr Andrea Haas *42*

Have You Ever Looked At Someone And Thought "I Wish I Was That Confident?" 43

Anni Jakenfelds *48*

What If I Told You That Lacking Confidence Was Making You Ill ! 49

Molly Jones MSc *54*

What If I Tell You That No Matter What Happens, You've Got What It Takes To Deal With It? 57

Claudia R Knights *62*

What If You Woke Up Tomorrow With Zero Confidence? . 65

Mats Kolbjornsen *70*

What If I Told You Even The Most Confident People Have Practiced To Become Confident? 71

Christine Laidlaw *76*

How Can You Increase Your Confidence With Pilates? ...79

Mike Lawrence *86*

What If I Told You That I Was The First Black Redcoat In The UK, And On Arrival, I Was An Introvert And Low In Confidence? 89

Jane McDowell *94*

The Pain/Confidence Connection. 95

Lisa Moore *100*

Lack Of Confidence Is Like Driving Through Life With Your Hand Brake On!. 101

Irma Prins. *106*

What If I Told You That Positioning Children Well, Gives Them Confidence And Independence? 109

Simon Rogers. *114*

Growing Your Unshakable Confidence 115

David Roylance *120*

If Barack Obama Can Be President, So Can You!. 121

Sophie Thwaites *128*

Increasing Confidence In Children By Building A Stronger Foundation 129

Bonus Chapter *135*

Building Confidence By Focusing On The One Area Most People Avoid! 135

A Final Thought From The Author. *149*

11 Habits Of Mentally Strong People 149

Congratulations!. 156

About The Authors & HCB Publishing 159

HCB Publishing. 161

DEDICATION

To our families, our friends and all the expert authors included in this book.

We love you all and thank you for joining us on the mission of making a difference in this world!

FOREWORD

Powerful Wisdom from leaders in the world of Confidence!

Experts are to be admired for their knowledge, but they often remain unrecognised by the general public because they reserve their information and insights for paying customers and clients. There are many experts in any given field, but their impact is limited to the handful of people with whom they work.

This book we hope in part, will change that. It brings together information that would not otherwise be available to the public so that more people can benefit from this expertise. We have specifically chosen experts with a unique experience and story to share so that this information is both accessible, actionable and will support as many people as possible.

Many experts have always dreamed of writing a book to share their expertise and 'superpowers' with the world. Becoming an author however, is a significant undertaking that not everyone turns into a reality. By providing their expertise and contributing to this book, these experts have not only made their dreams a reality, they also offer a much richer experience of life for you, the reader.

We know not everyone has the same experience of Confidence and by combining these experts insights and experiences, we hope that you will find yourself in these pages and be able to gain insight, inspiration and perhaps solve your own challenges in this area.

We know that you will learn a lot from reading these chapters and connecting with these experts. Enjoy!

Chris & Karene Lambert-Gorwyn and David Gil Cristobal

Bestselling and Award-Winning Authors

INTRODUCTION

Unlike most books that you might read, this is not a theoretical treaty or fictional discussion of what may or may not work. It is real experience from real people making a real difference that can apply to you own life and circumstances, if you take action.

Bringing together expertise and advice usually reserved for high-paying clients, this book will give you insights, inspiration and most importantly actions so you can make a difference in your life today.

All of the contributing authors have many years of experience, countless successes and of course, a fair few failures. Many of them experienced challenges personally, or had clients or family members who have inspired their journeys and they're now on a mission to share and make solutions, knowledge and experience accessible for more people.

So many people want to make a difference in the world and yet find themselves held back by fear and doubt. The people who have co-authored this book have overcome this to reach more people and make a bigger difference.

If you have picked up this book and have read this far, then you either want to know more or change something in your life. This means that you, like the authors of this book, will have to overcome your fears and doubts.

We know from neuroscience and first-hand experience from training thousands of people, that lasting change requires 3 key elements: the first is KNOWLEDGE, which you will find in these pages; the second is your MINDSET, which again this book will influence; and lastly a supportive COMMUNITY.

We hope you will find this community in the stories and experiences included in these pages. By their sharing their own experiences and the stories of those they have treated, supported and made a difference for, the authors will provide you with an all-important community of support for you to move forward.

You may recognise yourself or others in these pages and we hope that will inspire you to take action and make a difference. By stepping into our best selves and living our best life, we become the change we want to see in the world. Whilst we might feel insignificant as individuals, our collective powers are boundless, so keep reading and see what differences you might be able to create for you, your life, family and those around you.

Chris & Karene Lambert-Gorwyn and David Gil Cristobal

Bestselling & Award Winning Authors

CONFIDENCE

Confidence shapes how we interact with the world. It shapes our relationships with ourselves and others and it creates the boundaries of what we imagine is possible. When confidence is low or missing, it can create anything from minor day-to-day stress, to extreme anxiety or overwhelming panic. For this reason, as well as many other reasons, it is vital to understand and balance the two components of confidence:

1. What we show to the world: External Confidence
2. What's actually going on inside us: Internal Confidence

Internal confidence is how you feel on the inside and external confidence is the perception that others have of you. Both of these are equally important and can be impacted and influenced by many different things. Yet unfortunately, for many people, internal and external confidence are not equally balanced leading to internal conflict and self-doubt.

For many years, as a result of bullying at school, external confidence was my only focus. It was my way of dealing with a situation I couldn't make sense of. It was critical to me that what I projected externally to the world was my version of 'perfect'. This came at a massive emotional and physical cost where I created a self-harming eating disorder. Whilst extreme and totally self-sabotaging, it meant I could control myself and create 'arms-length' relationships, so I could feel in control the narrative. And all this so that I could perpetuate an internal need to 'succeed' and 'look good' in the world. As coping mechanisms go, whilst being emotionally and physically damaging and not something I would recommend, they served me well in creating success in my career.

However, with this focus on external confidence, and the ensuing trauma it created, I eventually realised I needed to develop my internal confidence and create true balance. So, after a lot of work and many years later, my internal confidence now matches the external perception the world has of me....well, most of the time anyway ;-)

It is from this experience of developing myself, combined with the experience of training thousands of experts and business owners how to succeed, that I share the suggestions I make below. Focusing on these key areas will allow for the development of your internal alongside your external confidence and therefore start the journey to creating better life results as well as a much happier head-space to be in. Using these suggestions along with the stories, insights and action steps outlined by the other experts in this book you'll find yourself well on your way to creating a level of confidence and self-assurance that is truly life changing.

Posture

How you stand impacts how you feel and most definitely the impression you give others. If someone is standing hunched over, shoulders drooped and looking at the floor, what would you instantly think about their mental and emotional state? You'd think they're depressed right? This will come across in their voice, they're mannerisms and everything they do. And they definitely would not come across as a leader or someone with confidence.

Instead, we need to stand or sit tall. This doesn't mean stiff military posture, nor does it have any reference to how tall you are. Standing tall means standing up within yourself.

Think of it more as being lifted by a bit of string attached to the top of your head. Your head raises and gently pulls the rest of your body up with it whilst remaining relaxed. By lifting the body by the head and remaining relaxed, we fully inhabit our space and have more presence. By looking up, lifting our head and our body; it impacts our thoughts and emotions and we release a whole new biochemistry of endorphins to lift us internally as well as externally.

Voice

Your voice is a very powerful tool and for many of us, it is underutilised or taken for granted.

As an international speaker presenting on stages all over the world, I am only too aware of the importance and the power of voice. Our voice, so much more than the words we use, is what people connect to and judge us by.

There are 3 key voices for effective communication in life and business. We need to be able to flow between these three voices depending on the situational requirements. Being able to move effectively between the 3 voices creates external confidence, whilst also boosting your own feelings of control therefore increasing internal confidence.

The 3 Voices are:

The Warrior Voice: This is the voice of command and

direction

The warrior voice is a deeper voice and is expressed in clipped sound bites such as commands. It doesn't need to be loud, because like all true authority if you have to shout, you don't have the authority. Instead, it is direct and very clear. There is no ambiguity or vagueness in the warrior voice.

The Heart Voice: This is the voice of connection and rapport

The heart voice is rounded, softer and warm. It's the type of voice you would use in a heartfelt conversation with a friend or someone you care for. This is the voice that says,

"Come in, I've just put the kettle on."

The Head Voice: This is the voice of excitement and energy

The head voice is higher pitched and faster-paced than the other voices. It's high energy and would be the voice you naturally use when talking to a child about an exciting activity. The head voice has energy and is infectious. The person listening will also feel energised, excited and uplifted by hearing it.

Energy

The biggest similarity between the successful people I've spent time with is their level of energy. The multimillionaires, the billionaires, the Olympic athletes, the entrepreneurs, the hugely successful people from many different walks of life....they all have huge amounts of energy and focus on what they're doing. This energy is palpable when you meet these people in person or over the phone and it infects everyone around them in the same way a smile does.

When you meet someone with that level of focus and energy, it releases something in you too. Without necessarily realising it, you start to step up more, aspire to achieve more and start taking bigger actions. This is vital in any leadership position as people will feed off your energy. People with energy always come across as confident and having more certainty and the great thing is, by projecting energy in your actions and conversations with people, your internal energy and confidence will raise to match it.

Smile

Smiles are what connect us universally with other humans. A smile tells the other person, "I am non-threatening and it is safe to connect." Of course, this only refers to genuine heartfelt smiles. We can all spot the phoney, pasted-on politicians smile a mile off and it doesn't do anything to connect us to the other person. However, the real deal, where someone is smiling from the inside can light up a room and is contagious in a way that people can't help but respond in kind. Smiling is a super-power when it comes to creating connection with other people. The better we connect with the people around us, the more confidence we project and the more confident we feel.

Please use these steps, along with the stories, suggestions and expertise offered by the other authors in this book, and like me, you'll create a massive difference in both your internal and external confidence.

And as an added benefit, your headspace will become a much happier place to spend time in!

Enjoy!

Karene Lambert-Gorwyn

Growing Heart Centred Businesses from Passion to Profit

Phone: +44 (0)333 987 4245

Website: www.chrisandkarene.com

Email: karene@heartcentredbusiness

Karene is the bestselling author of Grow Your Heart Centred Business from Passion to Profit and considered the UK's #1 Business and Wealth Mentor. Living in London with her husband Chris and daughter Mya, Karene and Chris support Practitioners and Experts to build heart centred businesses where they make a bigger difference in the world and get paid what they're truly worth. Karene and Chris's clients typically increase their income by £50,000-£100,000 within 12 months of implementing their systems.

Jules Francis

Transforming Your Relationship With Food

Jules Francis is the go-to-expert for career-driven women who are looking to transform their relationship with food. She has helped hundreds of people from all walks of life to help them understand the underlying causes of why they over-indulge in food they know is bad for them and do it anyway.

Jules is an international speaker, passionate and committed to support those ready to improve their physical and mental wellbeing which ultimately leads to a happier, healthier version of oneself.

She sees clients face to face from her consulting room in Brighton where GP's and nurse practitioners refer their patients to her and sees UK and international clients online.

Jules has travelled the world, lived and worked in Italy and is a mother of two delightful daughters. They live by the sea in central Brighton together with their house rabbits.

Website: www.julesfrancis.com

Email: jules@julesfrancis.com

Phone: +44(0)7803 121 923

What If I Told You That Food Cravings Are Your Body's Way Of Communicating?

When the going gets tough what do *you* reach for? A jumbo bar of chocolate? An entire packet of biscuits? A bottle or 2 of wine?

What if I also told you that it could be down to a lack of confidence that leads to these compensating behaviours.

Whatever your reasons are for choosing the foods you eat, there are two driving factors: *hunger and desire.*

Most of our food cravings and choices have little to do with the actual food but instead are based on either our thoughts about food, something we learnt from someone else or simply a habit. However, when we stop and become more mindful, we start to build trust between our bodies and mind again and can then see the reasons behind our eating habits.

With three decades of working professionally with people from all walks of life, I have the insight to see what truly underpins low confidence and how people often choose compensating behaviours to deal with it. I feel fortunate to have helped hundreds of people discover the root causes of why they are over-indulging in unhealthy foods and how some of their negative beliefs may have played a part.

To help explain this further, I'd like to share with you how one of my clients binged on food she knew wouldn't help her waistline or energy levels but just couldn't say no. She was a lovely lady, a psychologist from Cyprus who continuously tried to please other people even if it made her unhappy. This pattern however usually followed with her feeling deflated and consequently would eat her way through a whole packet of shortbread biscuits.

When exploring this further, we discovered the root cause of her unhealthy eating patterns - being bullied at primary school because she didn't want to do what her friends were doing. It was this underlying fear of being bullied again that led to a subsequent lack of confidence. Once she released this fear, she was then able to discover a better way forward, regardless of what others thought. I'm delighted to tell you that she can now stop at just the one shortbread biscuit and relishes each mouthful.

Being able to recognise when your body is rejecting something should be easy to say no to it next time. So why is it so hard to say no? Usually it is sign that there are some unidentified emotions deep beneath the surface.

I'd like you to picture yourself shopping for food. Watch as you take an item off the shelf and put it in your trolley. Remember it will then be taken to your kitchen and what is in your kitchen will ultimately be eaten. Have you made a good choice for your body? If not, what is it that drove you to that choice?

Take a moment to pause, breathe and reflect. With mindful breathing you can slow down the chitter chatter in your mind that may say things like 'I don't deserve good things', 'I'm not good enough for that' 'I'm not worthy of anything better'. It's these limiting belief patterns that may make you reach for that unhealthy food from the supermarket shelf in the first place. We all have these voices in various degrees so once again, you are not alone!

Every year, I take my children to a mindfulness retreat called Plum Village in South West France. We spend a few weeks enjoying the simple things that are so easily taken for granted in everyday life. Cleaning teeth is a great time to be mindful as is chopping vegetables, walking - mindfully placing one foot in front of the other or eating a meal. During these incredible retreats, we are all reminded that our daily tasks can be powerful moments for self-reflection and a chance to be in the present moment.

Something worth remembering is this: You don't need to go anywhere to come back to the present moment. It's here. Right now. With practice, you feel rejuvenated, fresh and alive which is a great foundation for building self-confidence. Like anything however, Rome wasn't built in a day, so be patient with yourself and just take small repetitive action steps daily.

Having confidence comes from a mindset that says I can, *I will, I am* and has a determination about it. It also comes from having little or no fear of rejection, failure or judgement and instead has an attitude of 'Well if I don't try, I won't know'.

A client who had lost that determination was a project manager from London who shared how confident he *used to be* and all the opportunities he benefitted from growing up. However, since losing his mother to cancer 3 years ago, he lost his focus in life and he felt flat. Sadly, this enormous loss caused him to develop new unhealthy eating habits such as skipping meals and snacking regularly on junk food instead.

He was wise not to let his new habits get too out of hand before asking for my support. During our sessions together, he recognised that he had un-resolved grief. Once when he had acknowledged these feelings and come to terms with what had happened in his own way, then he was able to celebrate his mothers' life and re-focus once again. Naturally, he then changed his eating habits more easily and the cravings for junk food disappeared.

Can you see how even though this appeared to be only a food related problem, reading a book on nutrition would not have reached the outcome he needed for a long-term solution? I spoke to him just last week and I was happy to hear that he became engaged, was promoted at work and his new favourite past time is cooking healthy meals for his fiancé.

Fortunately, as you can see by this example, confidence can be re-built, strengthened and encouraged to grow so whilst you might be someone who is confident in one area of your life, you may lack confidence in another.

In addition to mindful breathing, another simple way of feeling more confident all round is by making eye contact when in conversation with someone else, relaxing your shoulders and standing tall. Our bodies naturally hunch over when we feel insecure and we tend to look down instead of ahead. Try it next time and see how different you feel.

You might be curious to know what your body is trying to communicate through your food cravings. Unfortunately, there isn't a simple formula such as craving X = lacking in Y when it comes to emotions but there is when it comes to lacking in nourishment.

Download my free '8 Causes of Cravings' gift here: http://julesfrancis.com/webinars/confidence-book/ **and see if you can understand your body better and what it really is asking you for.**

If you are then keen to explore what underpins your own relationship with food, book yourself in for a free 30 minute coaching call and let's find a way for you to have a healthy relationship with food once and for all: https://julesfrancis.as.me/MovingForward

Anna Goodwin

Managing Director of Heart Centred Business

Anna Goodwin excels at helping people get out of their own way, so that they can get unstuck in their lives and businesses. Mumpreneur and Managing Director at Heart Centred Business, Anna trains experts how to make a bigger difference in the world and get paid what they're truly worth.

A former Secondary School teacher who left teaching to set up her own successful enterprise, Anna helped hundreds of women overcome anger and regain a spring in their step. Watching the women she supported regain their passion for life and step into their true potential led Anna to bring her expertise to the award-winning company Heart Centred Business in the role of Managing Director. With clients typically achieving £50,000-£100,000 growth within 12 months of implementing their systems, Anna and the Heart Centred Business team support women to create an income, a business and a mindset beyond anything they believed to be possible.

Anna Goodwin

Website: www.heartcentredbusiness.com

Email: anna@heartcentredbusiness.com

Phone: +44(0)3339 874 245

Do You Feel Confident In Sales?

What do you think of when you hear the word Sales? Does it have you jumping for joy at the idea of being able to serve someone or do you feel icky inside or want to run for the hills?

I'm Anna Goodwin, the Managing Director at Heart Centred Business, where we train experts how to make a bigger difference in the world and how to turn their passion into profit and I have the particular pleasure of spending a good proportion of my days selling... and I love it!

The story I would like to share with you starts when I was 21, fresh out of university having studied Textiles. My father, who is retired now and well, was at the time recovering from cancer. The family jewellery business was suffering from the repercussions of his illness, sales were significantly down and a sales representative was needed. So I swapped my 'arty' student attire for a pukka MaxMara suit, killer heals and lipstick. Dad trained me up as best he could and off I went, with my huge sample bag of silver, gold and diamonds galore in tow. I was set for great success - or so I thought.

The reality was that even though I knew in theory how to sell jewellery, I felt totally out of my comfort zone - with the added weight of the family business my shoulders. On the surface, I was up for the challenge, and yet, deep down I was unbelievably nervous, like a rabbit in head lights.

Most of the jewellery shops I sold to, were old family business, run predominately by old grumpy and rather intimidating men. They had been used to dealing with dad for 20 years... and then his daughter showed up, young, clearly inexperienced and lacking in confidence - and oh boy, did they test me.

They wanted to know every single little detail of every process of every product: From the precise origins of the diamonds and stones to the thickness and sizes and methods of production. I actually knew most of the answers, but if I did not know my 'stuff' then they would not buy. It put me on the back foot, and I always felt I had a lot to prove. Needless to say, I did not enjoy the sweaty palms, rushing heart beats and knotted tummies of those 3 years - and by the end I swore I would never sell again.

Fast forward 12 years: Married, a secondary school Art teacher with two children, I turned my attention to starting my own business - StressFreeMums. It was an area I was super passionate about. Helping mums like me, who had suffered severely with stress, anxiety and overwhelm.

There were many obstacles I came across trying to get my business off the ground - and for the purposes of this chapter I'll stick to my reluctance to sell!

I was happy in my skills, in finding out what the problem was and how I could help them long term. The downside was, I was massively lacking in confidence and actively avoided talking about money- how to invest in themselves and to actually move forward! Instead, I would send them a follow up e-mail after a consultation, with costs and leave them to make a final decision on their own.

The results were, well, what do you think? In those four years I hardly helped any mums in the way that I could have done. There are all sorts of reasons, excuses and stories why I didn't talk about money: they all came down to a lack of training and a need for a massive shift in mindset. I left my potential clients, while already in heaps of overwhelm, to a make a big decision of a signifiant investment on their own.

It's not that I didn't help anyone during this time, but clients were few and far between. I also wanted to help create long term solutions by getting to the route of their problems. Typically, clients would come to see me when they were in a 10/10 overwhelm: I could help them with this - no problem, but as soon as they got back down to their bearable 8/10 pain again, where they had often been for years - I would't see them again. Not the long term results they or I wanted! ... partly because I never connected with greater value that working with me would have on the rest of their life.

I was about to throw the towel in on my business when I found myself in a room with 50 other practitioner businesses on a 3days training, teaching us the blue-print of how to earn 6 figures from our passion... including how to sell in a heart centred way!

Over the next few years I followed their systems, taking plenty of actions to help my business grow. When it came to learning how to sell however, there were 2 key areas that made all the difference.

1. **Knowledge** - There IS a real Heart Centred sales system to learn and practice so that you and the client feel like its Win/Win all the way! The down side is that it still does not feel like this until you

work on the....

2. **Mindset** - I was still having body reactions, similar to those when I was selling jewellery all those years ago. Needless to say there was a fair amount detective work to be done. I'm not alone in having a fear of being judged, or being rejected, or stepping into being a leader, but it super unhelpful in sales if these are the 'blocks' standing in your way and in the way of your client getting the help they need! Oh yes, and I also had a whole heap of self sabotaging patterns and stories about what money meant to me! What an eye opener uncovering these were!

Over the next 4 years, I grew my business exponentially before being offered the incredible opportunity to become the Managing Director of Heart Centred Business. We have had the privilege of supporting over 3000 other practitioner businesses on a same-same, but different journey. It's not often someone doesn't massively benefit from changing their knowledge and Mindset around Sales and Money.

'Experience is a hard teacher because she gives the test first, the lesson afterwards' Vernon Law. Selling jewellery was my test and it's only now I can look back with fondness, knowing it was nothing to do with what I was selling, or who I was selling it to - but instead to do with my mindset and inner confidence. If I went back to sell jewellery now I know it would be a totally different experience. However, selling a luxury product verses selling a transformation of someones business, and their life - for the rest of their life: This is what really excites me now!

If my story resonates with you, do go now and get some proper heart centred sales training. Sales, it turns out is just service! And serving is something we can all do. If I can get over myself; with the right knowledge, the right mindset and the right community, even the most reticent of us can start to get amazing results and feel confident when we sell something. If you are curious about the experiences that I have been sharing here - please do be in contact now, we would love to explore what might be possible for you too.

If you would like to transform your sales there are several options to move you forward now:

* Buy the Amazon best selling HCB book - which includes is a huge section on sales and money for you to learn and practice from. www.heartcentredbusiness.com/book

* If you are in the business of helping others - I am happy to offer you a free strategy call now to help your business move forward. www.heartcentredbusiness.com/free-strat-call

- If you want to start a business journey, where you help more people and make more money. Go now to - 'Find your Passion and Earn your first £1000' - www.passiontoprofitforpractitioners.com/first-1000

Emma Grace

Emma Grace specialises in helping professional women in their 40s who are usually passionate and enthusiastic, but find life is feeling a bit "bleugh". Their body aches, work is tedious, and their relationships jangle – and they're frustrated because they know life can be so much better. Emma helps them feel younger than they have in years, excited and inspired at work, and happy in their relationships, so their lives are transformed in ways they couldn't have imagined. They go from "bleugh" to "WOOHOO!!!".

Diagnosed with a serious illness at 22, following a mere bout of 'flu, Emma was told by doctors that she would probably spend the rest of her life in bed. The illness took her whole life with it, but Emma was determined her future would be better. So she threw herself into learning everything she could about health and wellbeing. She slowly, slowly, learnt her way back to health. It took 10 years.

Starting from scratch in her early 30s, Emma was well but life was a bit...bleugh. She kept looking, studying and successfully working with many clients with challenges in life and health. It took a long time...but she found her WOOHOO!!! Combining decades of experience to create her own system, Emma's clients now get the sort of journey to WOOHOO that she wishes hers had been.

Emma's driving belief is that each human being is unique and infinitely precious. The world needs the special thing that they bring, and they deserve to be the best of themselves – and well – and happy. WOOHOO!!!

Email: emmagracetherapy@gmail.com

Phone: +44(0)7392 079 646

How To Fly When Your Wings Are Broken

I guess you know, if you're reading this book, how incredibly vulnerable you feel when you lack confidence. It seems to be the worst thing about it – that, and the way it stops you doing stuff. So I'm going to be vulnerable with you, and tell you about how I went from having so little confidence I could barely talk to building my own therapy practice and presenting in public. The things I learnt on this journey form the core of what I do with so many clients, who come to me when life is just not quite working. Confidence is often a factor.

<u>You know when your wings get broken...?</u>

Once upon a time, I was flying in confidence. Ready to take on the world. But then a horrible illness struck. I was ill for 10 years, unable to get out of bed, see friends, work – even breathing could be a battle. Those years took with them almost everything: achievements, dreams, hopes, plans, joys, friendships, independence, dignity... identity... It is beyond a loss of confidence; it is a demolition of self. When I started getting out of the house again, I couldn't even count on my own body to get me from the room I was in to the car that was waiting; I fixed my eyes on the pavement as I walked, and shrivelled inside when passing strangers in the street; I found it hard to speak, even to my extended family, who are good people who love me.

Does some of this sound familiar to you? The world is in a different place from you. Your friends are achieving things you aspired to while you watch and cheer and... wish. There is stuff you're expected to know that you don't, and stuff you know that they can't imagine or begin to understand. You're just – different. Different from most other people. Different from what the world expects.

Let me tell you a secret: this is also your superpower, your gift to the world.

Where do you start when you have nowhere to start from? It's incredibly scary, but it's also very...liberating. You are free to experiment. So experiment. What have you always wanted to try but never got round to? What is just vaguely in your head? Or a passing fancy? Do it.

I'd lost so many opportunities, I decided to try everything that I possibly could. "Say 'yes' to everything" was one of the best pieces of advice I have ever been given. Lack of confidence had previously meant I tended to say no – but it's not even about confidence. It's because you know that life is too short not to live and breathe it. I suddenly found myself loving adventure sports, which was about the least "me" thing ever. Some things stuck (water sports), other things did not (thick slabs of boiled dough that glue your teeth together. I have no idea why that meal exists.). I was often quite rubbish at it, but I ended up meeting nice people and having fun. Find things that light you up. Fun. Laughter. Have you ever tried shuffling unconfidently while buzzing with adrenaline or crying with laughter?

Why have I started by talking about enjoying yourself, when life is full of responsibilities? Because you need a base level of OK to be able to function. It is an inescapable biological fact that your body and brain work better when you are happy. Imagine facing a challenge while you are howling with laughter or sparkling with joy. You see...? The thing is that when you're happy, even for a moment, confidence is not even a factor. It makes it easier to do stuff. So find things that make you happy.

What about responsibilities? Jobs were hard, because for a start, I had a medical history where my employment history should have been. And I didn't know what I wanted to do, exactly. And I didn't know what I had to offer. What did I know? (MUCH, MUCH more than I realised – and so do you.) From there, it was small, small, tiny steps. Do you find that tiny steps can feel like huge steps (or turn into a flipping mountain that takes forever to navigate)? That you beat yourself up about small steps – you want things to move much faster, feel you should be able to do better? The thing I'm learning is that if it feels like a huge step, it is a huge step. Even if it looks small on the outside, you have made massive progress inside by doing it, and you can build on that.

What hacks are there to help with this journey? You know one. It's the starting point above. It is so counter-cultural, though, that I spend my life reminding myself and my clients to do it. Have fun. Do things that bring you joy and peace.

I dance regularly – it gets me out of my head and fills me with natural happy chemicals. Sometimes I need a walk, or a duvet day, or a day sleeping in the sun (if we only have three sunny days a year, it seems a shame to waste them). I am ruthless in taking holidays: I take them, regularly, and switch everything off. Outside my work window is a bird feeder – little moments being lost in joy throughout the day.

So find lots of good things, and roll around in them like a dog in grass, in glorious abandon with a big grin on your face (if you want to wave your legs in the air, do that, too). The better we are nourished, the more we grow.

Another hack is this: your confidence issues are in your head. So use your body. Put the book down a moment and tell me: if you slouch over, roll your shoulders in, look down, how do you feel? And if you imagine you are being suspended by a golden thread from the top of your head, your shoulders open and relaxed, feet on the ground, breathing into your tummy, looking ahead and with a smile on your face, how do you feel? Your body feeds back to your brain, so you can up your confidence simply by changing how you hold yourself.

I once had to walk alone into a room and make a short presentation in front of hundreds of people. I was so afraid I couldn't think. Outside those doors, I focussed on my body. Got my posture right. Felt how Confident Emma moves. Breathed deep into my legs, feeling only my body and how it is grounded and assured. I reminded myself of two points I wanted to make, and I went. I delivered them. Barely thinking, staying in my body. Then I left, and hid in the toilets and gibbered, couldn't even remember what had just happened. When I came back, I was told I absolutely owned the room, I seemed so confident.

Use your body. It can change how you feel. It can change how others see you. So it can help you fake it – till you make it. And you will make it. You will become that person. Because that person is you – the liberated you.

Finding moments of joy, taking those tiny, faltering steps, looking after myself on the way, eventually led me to train in both mental and physical health. To develop my own model for treating people. To "become the catalyst for change", help people feel "better than I have for 20 years", to find the "miracle".

Taking those small steps, saying yes, getting into my body, led to me presenting, being the wellness expert on a recorded public panel, writing this book. Being this vulnerable. In public. In print. If you are starting out with broken wings, you know how hard that is.

And now you know you can get there – or somewhere equally unimaginable. And you know how. And you know you must, because you want to, because you are the only person in the world who brings what you bring and we need you, because you are reading this book and have taken the first step. What awesome thing will you do to make yourself laugh? And what is your next small step?

Fly.

If you would like to learn how to use your body and mind to step out into the world, live an amazing life, and stand proudly in the remarkable person that you are, get in touch with Emma for a free Coaching Session on 07392 079 646, emmagracetherapy@gmail.com.

Dr Andrea Haas

Health Happiness and Inner Strength

Surrey's holistic, medication-free approach to facial pain With over 30 yrs experience of working as a musculoskeletal doctor on the NHS, including working at the Royal London Hospital for Integrated Medicine, in private practice and for the army, Andrea has a wealth of experience. More recently this has led her into working in Pain Management.

Over the last 15 years she has become more interested in the mind and its impact on the body. 10 yrs ago she branched out as a therapist realising that she could offer her clients so much more this way. Using a variety of tools, often described as a toolbox, Andrea works in a holistic way, helping her clients move forward, not just with their pain, but also in other areas of their lives.

Website: www.andrea-inner-strength.co.uk

Email: andrea@andrea-inner-strength.co.uk

Phone: +44(0)7770 672 122

Have You Ever Looked At Someone And Thought "I Wish I Was That Confident?"

You watch them and nothing seems to phase them, they appear as cool as a cucumber. I have! I suffered with a severe lack of confidence when I was younger. When I got to medical school it just seemed to get worse, and when I qualified, I would dread going out to the waiting area to call my patients. If I could avoid it, I would. The frustrating thing was, that it just seemed to get worse with time. However, I came up with a strategy. I found that if I started saying to myself over and over again "I am confident" just before I got up from my desk to go and call my next patient, I could prevent that negative voice in my head from being heard. But, back then, little did I know that many years later I would a learn a much quicker and more effective technique to help my clients. So, who am I?

I am Dr Andrea Haas and I love working with professional health conscious women, aged between 45 and 55 who suffer with persistent facial pain. So, why, I hear you ask, have I written a chapter in a book about confidence? Because suffering with persistent pain, of any kind can lead to a loss of confidence simply because pain causes you to do less. Whatever is causing your lack of confidence the principles of how to improve it are the same. As I found, all those years ago, it is about a little voice in your head telling you negative things. Have you ever heard that little voice?

All of us have a constant chatter in our heads, and if

you were to stop and listen to it, just for a minute you would be very surprised at how it talks to you! And it's not nice! It criticises, it berates, it calls you names. We rarely praise or encourage ourselves unless we have been taught how to do it. All these thoughts have an effect on how we feel, which then influences how we behave. It's not surprising, then that if our thoughts are negative it is going to produce negative emotions which influence our behaviour in a negative way. This behaviour then produces even more critical thoughts. Let's look at an example of this.

Let's say you're a nervous driver. Any thoughts you may have around driving will be negative, such as I'm going to have an accident, I won't be able to get out of that busy junction, people always cut me up. This anxiety affects how well you drive, and one day you nearly have an accident. This sparks even more negative thoughts which then makes you even more nervous about driving. One of my clients came to see me in a similar situation affecting his golf swing.

I had been suffering with complete negativity about my golfing ability. I could hit magnificent shots at the driving range, but as soon as I reached the golf course the "demons" arrived to haunt me, and I couldn't hit a decent shot at all. I had so many negative thoughts going on inside my head, I was even having trouble commencing my back swing for fear of what was going to happen next! After just one session with Andrea and listening to the session recording, she did over the past month, I have manged to get my game back on track and even reduce my handicap! Thank you so much, Andrea! You have done more for my game than any golf professional could have achieved.

CPM, Surrey.

So, it's a vicious cycle: negative thoughts and beliefs, such as "I can't do this", "it's all going to go wrong" influence what we think is going to happen, and this affects the outcome. If it does all go wrong, then this adds fuel to the fire of negative thoughts and beliefs, and we are then on the downward spiral of it never going right. Another client came to see me worrying about whether he would be able to complete a marathon.

I decided at the tender age of 50 to run a marathon. Training was intermittent due to injuries and niggles. Normally a confident person, I found myself doubting my ability and fearful that I couldn't accomplish my goal even contemplating withdrawing from the event. Just 2 sessions with Andrea in the final few weeks of training did the trick. I'm not sure what she did but on the day I felt confident and determined. I had only achieved 13 miles in training but completed the full 26 miles on the day and within the time I had set myself. I have never run this distance previously. All my niggles and fear melted away and not only did I finish, I thoroughly enjoyed the whole experience!

JD Surrey.

These two examples are sporting activities, but the same principles can be applied to any situation.

What can you do to help yourself improve your confidence?

Here are a couple of simple techniques that you can practise. And like all things that are new, it may seem awkward or challenging, but stick at it, because as you practise more and more it will become easier.

1. Pay more attention to any thoughts running

through your head. Start saying encouraging, positive things to yourself, such as “I can do this”, “it will all be fine”.

2. Do some daydreaming! Imagine the activity going well. Imagine the sounds you would hear, what you would see, what you feel, and the emotions you have. Make the picture as big and bright as possible and soak it up.

If you are interested in exploring how your pain may be affecting your confidence, why not contact me on 07770 672122 to arrange a free 45 min consultation to see how I may be able to help. There is no obligation to this session, however, by the end of it, I promise you will be excited to have clarity on the next steps you could take to reduce your pain and hence increase your confidence.

Anni Jakenfelds

Harnessing your Brain to Beat Burnout for Good

Over 10 years-experience working specifically with burn-out, Anni is a leader in her field. As a neuroscientist, researcher, therapist and meditation teacher, she combines a scientific approach with accessible holistic practices suitable for all levels of suffering.

In her private practice, international clients come from around the world. As a consultant within corporate organisations she provides mental wellbeing seminars and workshops to support improved employee health.

Anni shows people how to throw off the shackles of the inner critic, and access the power of the leader within, so that they too can possess confident lives full of radiant health and wellbeing.

Website: www.ihealprocess.com

Email: anni@ihealprocess.com

Phone: +44(0)7934 442 129

What If I Told You That Lacking Confidence Was Making You Ill !

The term 'low confidence' may read, on paper, like a seemingly small thing to deal with. In reality, it can be a serious and insidious problem, even impacting your mental and physical health. Feeling like your own brain is fighting a war against you. Sending out constant whispers of distrust until you shrink your life to accommodate the fears, and your body feels anxious and tired all the time. Having spent the last 10 years working with women suffering from long-term burn-out, I can confidently say that lacking trust, self-esteem and confidence was a key issue for them all... this author included.

To those that know me I am a confident and vivacious woman. However, this was not always the case. I was the very definition of a shy child. Constantly worried what other people would think, the confidence to speak up was just not a skill I possessed! This lack of confidence presented itself in some peculiar ways. I meticulously planned every step of being around other people, from checking menus online to ensure I knew what I would eat before going to a restaurant, to learning multiple routes to my destination in case I felt unsafe along the way. I stayed up all night contemplating how I had messed up, considering how I could make tomorrow better, safer, until one day when I was 16 years old my body could no longer hold it all in. On my commute to school, standing packed like a sardine on a rush hour train to Marylebone Station, my world went black.

My legs didn't want to help me stand. My ribcage felt

compressed, like the whole carriage was pushing itself into my chest, so that I couldn't take in more than a sip of breath. Each blink of my eyelids made shapes and colours disappear until there was no difference between my eyes being open or closed. One scared sentence was all I managed to get out, 'Dad, I can't see. anything.'. Then I crumpled like a dropped coat. I had had my first panic attack.

You would think this moment would have been a pivotal one, that I would have changed instantly for fear of further consequences. However, developing confidence in yourself doesn't always work like that. Instead my inner critic told me I hadn't been holding things together tightly enough, I needed to be more fastidious, more in control. So, for another six years I stayed stuck in my ways. That said, something had shifted; my ears were now pricked by information on panic attacks, anxiety symptoms, breathing styles, and relaxation techniques. I started to digest as much as I could, trying to understand what went on in my brain and body. Fast forward over a decade and now I can see how this moment crafted my life and my career. How this moment taught me that those inner voices can shape our health and wellbeing, for better or worse. And how important it is to ask women suffering from burn-out what they say to themselves when they think no-one is listening.

TOP TIPS

Hands up if you have ever been taught, specifically, how to be a confident human being. No? Then let's break it down into 3 simple tips that I use with great success in my own clinic to help clients alleviate anxiety and take back control from their inner bullies.

1. Breathe Out

Using the breath is one of the most effective ways to calm a part of the brain known as the amygdala, AKA the fear centre. When we are feeling less confident, we typically breath from the upper portion of our chest and use the shoulder and neck muscles more than is useful. Just like when I had my panic attack, you are left with very little ability to breath in or out fully. Not breathing out is a big problem.

This changes the oxygen levels in the body, which the amygdala receives as a potential threat and enhances an anxious physical response, like a racing heart, to try and fix the situation.

Action Point: Next time you feel your confidence slip, squeeze the tops of your shoulders up towards your earlobes, perhaps you can even make them touch, as you breath in. Then relax them down like heavy weights as you breath out. With every exhale, relax your jaw with a big sigh of relief, almost like you are letting go of a big morning yawn. Do this at least 3 times and repeat as frequently as you need to until you feel calmer and more confident.

2. Mix It Up

The term 'comfort zone' implies that we start making changes from a place of comfort, when typically, we seek change because of how uncomfortable our current situation is! If you believe that in order to change anything you will have to be even more uncomfortable, you are likely to experience a surge of fear. Do you make choices that keep things the same, despite wanting something different long-term? Narrowing your world dents your confidence and stops you supplying new information to a part of the brain known as the hippocampus, which is involved in how easily we learn and remember things.

Action Point: Consciously and consistently mix up your habits and do something unfamiliar, or new. Keep these small, actionable steps. Give yourself permission to keep it as comfortable as it needs to be to keep you moving forward; the best action plan is the one you actually do! Drive a new route to work, walk around the park the opposite way, sit in a different chair at the dinner table, cook a new recipe, move the furniture in your bedroom or living room. It can be simple to start. These easy actions can prepare you for the next steps and even bigger changes, helping shift your habits, adjust your perspective, and boost your confidence. Practice this regularly, and it might even enhance your memory!

3. Be Kind, Be Honest

There is a lot of talk about being positive as a remedy to anxious thinking. Sometimes this can be misconstrued as simply reversing negative thoughts, but false positivity is akin to lying to ourselves, and lies help no-one but the inner critic. A previous client, let's call her Maddy, told people she earnt 100k because she had been told to speak what they wanted into existence and it would happen faster. Maddy actually earnt less than 20k. She ended up in a lot of debt, crippling anxiety and didn't get the help that was right for her or the circumstances she was in. Do not lie to yourself and fake it until you make it; be kind, be honest and face it until you make it.

Action Point: To set you up for success, I have two powerful words for you to use in your daily vocabulary; 'learning' and 'yet'. This one is especially important for all perfectionists. Say out loud to yourself right now 'I love myself exactly as I am'. Which little voice answered that in your head? Did it feel honest to say it out loud or did your mind find a whole host of unhelpful little remarks to make? Now try, out loud, 'I am learning to love myself exactly as I am'. Just how easily do you feel the difference? One more time 'I do not love myself exactly as I am yet.'

The root of low confidence can be as unique as the individual experiencing it. However, across the board, it is exhausting to consistently think so little of yourself. When it comes to burnout, what I have seen most often is a traumatic moment causing a long-term loss of confidence. This can be something as seemingly small and innocuous as a negative comment by a teacher or parent, a physical accident such as car crash or emergency surgery, or an experience of abuse that stole the confidence they used to possess. If this resonates with you, or had you thinking of someone particular in your world, I offer a complimentary Exploratory Conversation to speak directly with me. This is valued at £250 but offered to you for free. If you recognise that lacking confidence has been holding you back, it would be my pleasure to hear your story, and discover the person you are longing to become!

Molly Jones MSc

Exercise Solution for Early Parkinson's

Helping people live well

Molly specialises in helping clients with neurological conditions, with 20 years of physiotherapy experience. She initially started her practice in the Philippines before moving to the UK in 2003. She has since worked for the NHS and privately, mostly in community-based settings. She's also holds Master's Degree in Chronic Conditions Management.

Molly understands that people with neurological conditions suffer with various symptoms such as weakness, pain, fatigue, difficulty with movement, and balance problems, as well as issues relating to mood, motivation, and confidence. She has specific interest in Parkinson's disease, falls prevention, and chronic fatigue syndrome.

Her main motto is to help people to live well despite having a long term condition. As an asthma sufferer, she has first-hand experience of how to manage, cope and adjust to the realities of a life-long condition, and she supports clients in developing their own coping strategies both physically and mentally.

Her programs are holistic and functional, designed to meet person-centred needs.

Website: www.abilityneurophysio.co.uk

Email: info@abilityneurophysio.co.uk

Phone: +44(0)7451 551 279

What If I Tell You That No Matter What Happens, You've Got What It Takes To Deal With It?

Restoring self-belief and living well – a journey with life-long conditions.

Mark was running as usual when he tripped and fell. His ankle was hurting so he thought best have it checked, just in case. He saw someone the next day, who noticed he also had tremor on his left hand. A few more appointments later, just a week before he was 57, he was told he had Parkinson's. He was about to retire at this point and found a holiday home in France. He had plans - holidays, endless golf sessions, time with grandchildren. What's going to happen to that now? How is the rest of his life going to turn out?

I've met a lot of people like Mark, people who were just getting on with their lives and then out of nowhere, got hit by a life-changing illness. He told me he felt a bit cheated by life, he worked hard for years and now he has to spend his retirement dealing with Parkinson's. Knowing there's no treatment and it will get worse over time, he felt lost and uncertain. Life will never be the same again. He didn't want to 'give in' to his condition, but he didn't know what to do. Everything felt out of his control.

Deep in our minds, we believe that we are in control over our lives and not the external forces beyond our influence. Feeling in control is a primal need that must be satisfied. Unfortunately, control is also the main thing that an illness can take away from us. When we're ill, we doubt our bodies and the world around us. We want to get better, yet we don't always know when that will be or how it will turn out, so we doubt our future as well. In Mark's case, he was most worried about how bad things will get over time. When we feel and think this way, it's hard to be optimistic. It's also easy to stay feeling sorry for ourselves, and continue with this viscous circle.

Self-doubt is as big a problem as physical symptoms, although for most of us, the latter would be the reason why we would seek help because we tend to focus on what we see, i.e. the physical body. Yes, it is important to work on recovery, strength, and movement, in fact, once we've dealt with physical problems, it will help us gain confidence. Just remember it's **also the other way around**. What do I mean by this? Well, have you ever been faced with a task then thought 'can I do this?' or 'what's the point?', and ended up not doing it? Our brains are very good at doing this as way of protecting us from the unknown. Mark had these moments many times – he asks, if things will get worse over time, why bother exercise? However, by doubting ourselves, we destroy our own hope. And if we have nothing to hope for, we wouldn't believe in our own possibilities.

Ok, so you're in a dark cloud and cannot see the blue sky called 'hope'. Let's go back in time, last few years or even further if you want. What's that like? What did you do? Where did you go? Who did you meet? What did you dream about? If, at the start, you find it hard to come up with something, take your time. This can be as short or as long as you want, after all, it's your life you're looking back into. See things for what they are, not worse or better. Then tell your story to yourself as if you are the young child you once were. This story is what you need to hold on to as you face the challenges ahead.

Let's go back to Mark's story. He's a funny, smart, and kind person. He's been happily married for 30 years, with 3 children and 8 grandchildren. He's had a successful working life and earned plenty of money as a result. He played golf at competitive level and was voted team captain twice in his club. Sadly, 5 years ago, he lost both his parents in a tragic car accident. As an only child and no siblings to share his grief with, he had to find the inner strength to move on, which he did. He had all of these qualities and experiences, and nothing would change that.

The point of this short exercise is to remind you that **you are not your condition, you are the person formed by your character, experiences, beliefs, values, hopes and dreams.** Illness does not rewrite your history, nor can it take away what you've already achieved. By reconnecting with who you are beyond your illness, you will find reason to hope. Celebrate and learn from all the things that happened in your life, and take this with you on your next journey.

Once you've completed this exercise and reconnected with who you are, you'll realise how many choices you've made along the way. And this carries on - **you can choose how you journey through your illness.**

Now this might sound odd when you are faced with a condition that will do what it wants to do over time. Yet, just like anything in life, we have a choice. Your condition will be part of your journey but it doesn't have to decide where you go. You decide where to go. You decide what you want to take with you and what you leave behind. If your body changes, choose to change with it. If it affects how you do things, choose different ways of doing it. Look at the choices around you, and if you don't like them, look again until you find the one that suits you.

You can also choose to be the victim, or you can choose to fight back. Sometimes, it's easier to be a victim, and wait for someone or something to save you. Just remember that by doing so, you are handing back control to your illness and consequently missing out on the chance to shape your own journey.

Mark chose to be in-charge. He knew that by staying fit, he had a better chance of fighting back Parkinson's. He decided to stop running, he played more golf instead which meant he was also walking more. They bought the house in France, which they will keep for as long as he can drive safely. We still work together to this day, 3 years on, because as his body changes, with a little help, he knows he can change with it safely and effectively. Mark has taken control of the things that he can, in the way that he can, so that Parkinson's doesn't decide his present and future.

By remembering who you are and what you're made of, you have every reason to believe you can shape your future, whatever your illness brings. You have a gift, talent, skill, knowledge, and experiences that makes you unique and capable of playing the cards that you're dealt with. You can define your own sense of normality, and you can change it to suit you. It really is up to you, and take pride in knowing that.

Summary for actions:

- Hope gives us courage and reason to carry on - what do you hope for?

- Reconnect with yourself beyond illness – what are you made of?
- Your choices will shape your journey – what will you choose?

If you, or someone you know, are struggling with self-belief whilst living with a life-long illness, let's now talk about it. Register for a consultation at www.abilityneurophysio.co.uk and let's see what's possible for you.

Hope is nearly as strong as despair, and greatly more pertinacious and enduring —Walter Savage Landor

Claudia R Knights

London's most compassionate sleep specialist

Claudia is passionate about helping women sleep well. Claudia typically works with female solicitors, who are struggling to sleep, which leaves them too exhausted to perform well at work or to enjoy time with their family and friends. She helps them regain control of their bodies and reclaim their sleep so that they have the energy to thrive in their daily lives. Claudia's unique approach combines her expertise in craniosacral therapy with over a decade of experience teaching meditation classes and workshops. She helps clients get the sleep they need to feel empowered to flourish in their careers and delight in the moments they spend with their loved ones.

Claudia's introduction to complementary therapies began 17 years ago. At the time, she was pursuing a successful corporate career when she was struck with grave health issues that conventional medicine struggled to resolve. Her journey through an array of therapies led to craniosacral therapy, which made such a monumental difference to her quality of life that she was inspired to become a registered therapist herself.

Claudia also continues to work as a Development Director for the charity, Impetus, which helps young people from disadvantaged backgrounds get the support they need to succeed in school, work and life.

Claudia holds a Master of Engineering in Aeronautics and Astronautics. She is an enthusiastic student of Iyengar yoga and lives and works in London.

Email: claudia@claudiarknights.com

What If You Woke Up Tomorrow With Zero Confidence?

"I have over 25 years of experience in my career! I know what I'm doing, why have I lost my confidence?" Jo had a successful career in the financial sector and came to my clinic to improve her sleep. She asked me this question in one of our sessions. While we can develop our capabilities to be expert in a given area, we may still lack the confidence to deal with life's challenges. Thankfully, we can all nurture and increase our confidence. How? We focus on developing the clarity of mind and creativity to find solutions to our challenges and building the belief that we *can* make life decisions. Jo's story shows how this approach transformed her life.

Jo thought her poor sleep was a result of her age and the effects of post-menopause and had accepted that this would now be her pattern of sleep. Through our work together, it became clear that Jo felt stuck and reluctant to engage in the conversations that she knew she needed to have both at the office and with her husband, to change aspects of her professional and personal life. Jo was a strong, capable and determined woman and was perplexed that at this stage in her life, she lacked the confidence to do this.

I helped Jo recognise that when we are sleep deprived, our ability to interpret others' facial expressions is impaired. While we can understand emotions like anger, fear, surprise, the more nuanced emotions like happiness and sadness are more challenging to identify. We then encounter tension and conflict in our social interactions because we miss these important social cues. I often see clients lose the confidence to deal with challenging or emotional matters when they experience this pattern repeatedly. For some, it impacts their confidence more generally.

As Jo's sleep began to improve, her confidence returned. By the end of our programme, Jo had several conversations about implementing the changes she wanted in her life. Interestingly, she didn't find them as difficult as she had anticipated. So what began as a conversation about getting better sleep, resulted in a life transformation for Jo, because she developed the confidence and clarity to address the issues that had her feeling stuck.

Lack of sleep can also impact our confidence to make crucial decisions. With insufficient sleep, the part of the brain responsible for rational thought and reasoning is overruled by another part of the brain, the amygdala. The amygdala is the reason we experience fear when we encounter things outside of our control. In this place of fear, we can lack the clarity to make the decisions that help us move forward in life. Tina was in her late 30s when she came to see me. She felt stuck and lacked the confidence to change her situation. Tina had struggled with depression and insomnia since she was a teenager, so I recommended that she might want to work with a counsellor as talking therapies would also help with her depression. The idea of talking therapy filled Tina with dread and was not something she felt she had the confidence to do. Through our work together, Tina began to see improvement in her sleep, announcing in one of our sessions that she had decided to start talking therapy. Importantly, she started those sessions. With better sleep, Tina was able to build the confidence she needed to take a giant step in her healing journey and to change her life.

Research shows that if we are consistently sleeping less than six hours, we are sleep deprived, which amplifies the amygdala response by 60%. Immediate gratification is the primary focus of this part of our brain. It will take decisions to satiate this need, whether they are sound decisions or not, so our risk-taking increases dramatically. We become unable to react appropriately or see the bigger picture in unexpected situations. A few nights of shorter sleep reveals little effect, but as the sleep deprivation builds over several nights, we take more significant risks with no perception of the difference from our normal state of mind. For one of my clients, Tom, this was seriously affecting his relationship with his partner and his career.

Tom came to see me as he was struggling with anxiety and disrupted sleep. Tom's behaviour had also become impulsive, and he was worried that he was on the verge of losing both his partner and his job. Tom had started taking medication under the supervision of his Doctor to help with the anxiety, and also wanted to address the destructive tendencies, but struggled to change. He had considerable responsibility in his work and needed to make commercial decisions, which now presented a problem, as he was taking unnecessary risks that would cost him his job. His daily experience manifested in a lack of confidence around making decisions which increased his anxiety. He felt trapped in a vicious cycle and couldn't see a way out. Tom's concentration also suffered, further impacting his confidence. A lack of sleep affects our focus, so we're unable to make meaningful progress with the task at hand. If we continuously struggle with an activity that we know we are capable of doing, we can be susceptible to self-doubt. As my work with Tom progressed, he was able to improve the quality and length of his sleep. He soon began to operate with a more level-headed and rational approach, and gradually, his confidence returned in his decision-making ability.

My years of experience with clients like Jo, Tina and Tom and my struggle with confidence have informed the unique system I use to support clients. Lacking confidence had been a feature of much of my life. While many would say that I appear externally confident, those who know me well are all too aware of my past difficulties. They would often see the overwhelming internal battle to overcome insecurity and the negative internal narrative that stopped me from enjoying so many experiences and suffering the regret of missed opportunities. For me, this lack of confidence manifested as fear of failure and embarrassment, keeping me frozen in hesitancy that at some level, I thought would keep me safe. In the past, feeling tired or exhausted was my normal state and I would be stuck with indecisiveness over the smallest of issues, struggling to develop the enthusiasm to explore new possibilities, not trusting that I knew which direction to take.

Through these experiences, I know first-hand the impact that better sleep has had on my confidence. I'm passionate about helping people sleep well so that they can restore their bodies and minds and have the vitality to feel empowered to flourish in their daily lives. And what do I still do today to sleep well and help boost my confidence? Here are three tips to get you started:

1) Set your clock! - It's essential to go to bed and wake up at the same time every day to combat that feeling of permanent jet-lag without the flight.

2) Meditate! - According to research conducted by Harvard, meditation is the second most effective self-help method we can use to improve our sleep. (The most effective method? See tip 1).

3) Kick the habit! - There are many lifestyle hacks to help us improve sleep. Avoiding caffeinated drinks from mid-afternoon, and for me, that means tea, has improved the quality of my sleep tremendously.

If you are struggling with a lack of confidence and poor sleep and would like to know how you can make the transition from feeling stuck to feeling confident and empowered to make changes in your life, email me at claudia@claudiarknights.com to arrange a complimentary 30-minute call.

Mats Kolbjornsen

London's Favourite Confidence Specialist for the Creative Professions

Mats Kolbjornsen specialises in helping you build your confidence, resourcefulness and sense of control. His experience working in mental health and management spans two decades, having run support and development services for individuals and third sector charity organisations.

With a background in psychology and music, Mats now typically works with creative professionals and entrepreneurs, whose confidence and self-belief might be getting in the way of their ability to take their work to the next level. He helps them become confident in their own abilities, to break through their potential perceived limitations, to share their passion and to create the life that they want for themselves.

Mats' own passion for psychological wellbeing, combined with a keen interest in entrepreneurship and the arts, has enabled him to work internationally with a myriad of organisations, charities and individuals, through workshops, talks, training, 1-to-1 work and research.

Website: www.matskolbjornsen.com

Email: getintouch@matskolbjornsen.com

Phone: +44(0)7561 442 661

What If I Told You Even The Most Confident People Have Practiced To Become Confident?

Practice Makes Confident!

I would like you to consider this. Consider you could confidently speak in front of hundreds or thousands of people. Consider you could speak in front of this audience about what you have created – your idea, your concept. Consider you could talk confidently about yourself and your story. Right now.

Now, imagine you used to dread it. For a brief moment, consider that you would shake like a dry leaf at the prospect. Even thinking about it would make you tense up and break out a sweat. Consider you would simply freeze up if you were asked to introduce yourself in any situations where there were one or more people present. This used to be me. I spent years developing a great ability to be fearful in situations where I had no need to be.

More importantly, this used to be Sophie. She grew up thinking and feeling that no one would be interested in her or what she had to say. She became so good at training herself to look out for any opportunities to have this belief confirmed. This is often what our mind does. Our mind serves to protect us, and although it would arguably be better if Sophie had grown up believing in herself, allowing her much more freedom to realise her potential much earlier on – any opportunities to speak up would confirm her fear of doing so. Her mind and body would remind her of previous awkward moments of speaking in class, and her physiological responses would remind her that she felt under threat whenever the opportunity for any such events arose. So, in this way she was kept protected – she was kept away from situations where she could have the possibility of changing this belief, and of having the opportunity to realise and notice that she could do something about it.

That is until one day she decided that she was not going to let this affect her in the same way any longer and she got in touch with me. You see, as well as having become skilled at protecting herself, she had also developed a great passion – a passion for creating magnificent artwork, concepts, ventures and ideas. Understandably, she wanted others to know about this and to be able to share her passion and work with others. For this to happen, she knew she would have to change things, so that she could promote herself, to introduce her ideas, and for others to appreciate and invest in her and what she had to offer.

Through the two of us working together, she was able to make powerful shifts and to train her mind in a much more productive way – a way that would enable her to remain calm, focused and in control. This ultimately allowed for her to be exposed to opportunities that would confirm that these situations could make her feel great, empowered and proud of herself. Most importantly, it finally allowed her to be able to share her passion with the world. So, instead of Sophie going through her life thinking and believing no one would be interested in her abilities, she is now an incredibly skilled and accomplished international artist and entrepreneur – spending her professional time doing what she loves and impacting society in a much more positive, profound and meaningful way.

Now, if you want to, *you* can also do this. In many ways we become what we practice. So, I encourage you to practice the following simple psychology strategy: Close your eyes. Imagine that you are in a situation, or just before a situation, where you want to be really good. Maybe this is just before a meeting, just before a talk, just before a social situation, or just before a performance. Then take yourself through the whole experience with you being and feeling fantastic. The way our mind works is that if we generate pictures, thoughts and feelings about the future where we are doing great – this significantly increases the probability that we do so. Subsequently, we start to look for more evidence to support this positive belief. On the other hand if we keep on seeing, hearing and feeling things in our imagination happening in a less beneficial way, we tend to look for evidence to confirm this instead.

Consequently, we really want to focus on training our minds to seek out, and therefore make good things happen. So, as we become what we practice, imagine going through this situation and allowing it to unfold just the way you want it to. Find yourself seeing the great things that you are doing, find yourself hearing positive feedback and sounds, and find yourself feeling calm, yet energetic, comfortable and confident in yourself – ready for anything that comes your way. Practice this frequently, and you will train your brain to filter through more of what is going to be helpful for you to make positive things happen. Taking this a step further, imagine having access to the control room of your mind, where you can adjust any and all the controls that govern how you think, feel and act –

making any tweaks and alterations that you want so that you have the perfect set of tools and resources you need in any given situation. You can, through practice, allow yourself to be the person you really want to be. Does that sound good?

Now, why am I telling you this? Ever since the day we were born, we have been influenced by how we process and interpret what happens around and within us. From the moment we enter into existence, and arguably long before that, we absorb things that can affect us and influence us. If we allow it, this has the potential to influence us from that point forward and potentially indefinitely.

Imagine for a moment that you are formed as an idea. Imagine then that this idea gradually begins to grow, to take shape. The idea starts to formalise, to materialise, and ultimately becomes a reality. That reality then enters the world and instantly begins to experience and to be influenced by what surrounds them. That reality has already become a person; a person that continues to perceive and to gradually attempt and succeed in making sense of what they are experiencing. From here on, this can go in an infinite number of directions. It is then up to us what we do with it.

Sophie was provided with opportunities to practice feeling good in situations that she used to find challenging, and one of my greatest passions is to help other people choose what they do with their experience. It is remarkable and amazing to have the chance to be alongside people on this journey.

It is for this reason that through working with my clients over the years, I have developed a unique 3-step process to help you go from where you are now to where you want to be – to finally become the confident person you wish and deserve to be.

Curious to explore taking the first step?

In that case, I have an exclusive, free bonus for you! Simply go to the following link now:

www.matskolbjornsen.com/anthology-book-bonus/

See you there.

Christine Laidlaw

Pilates & Movement Specialist

Christine Laidlaw is a mumpreneur, Pilates and Movement Specialist and Director of The Chatsworth Studio a Pilates and wellbeing studio in Cheam Village in Surrey, England.

Christine has had a successful career in financial I.T. support. During this time Christine had a car accident, which damaged her back and caused a long-term whiplash injury. Pilates helped her to recover, repair her back and become pain free. A passionate convert to the benefits of Pilates she quit her job in I.T. to train as a Pilates teacher. This enabled her to pursue her ambitions of building her own business at the same time as creating a better work/life balance and to raise a family.

The Chatsworth Studio has grown from its initial beginnings in her dining room at home into church halls and finally to a modern, well equipped pilates and wellbeing Studio.

In her 20 years of practice she has helped hundreds of her clients resolve their back pain, increase their energy and improve their confidence.

Website: www.chatsworthstudio.com

Email: christine@christinelaidlaw.com

Phone: +44(0)7814 003 679

Facebook: @chatsworthstudio

Twitter: @chatsworthstudi

Instagram: chatsworth.studio

How Can You Increase Your Confidence With Pilates?

What is confidence? Do you feel sure of yourself and your abilities? It may be that you are very good at one area of your life and not so strong in another. I can get people out of pain and get them to feel confident in their own bodies by teaching them Pilates, but if you asked me to guide a mountaineering group to the Himalaya's I wouldn't be able to do it. Stepping out of your comfort zone once in a while is good for all of us and keeps us challenged mentally and physically! It may be that you lack confidence when trying something new, such as giving a presentation, learning something new or trying a new exercise class. I have had to present a Dragons Den style presentation recently and it was incredibly scary. It was out of my comfort zone. There were approximately 60 people on Zoom all looking at me and I had to sell my specialism and business to the investors! Even though I was nervous I had realised preparation and breathing were key. It was a success and the presentation went well. It is always good to try new things. I have included two of my client stories below to demonstrate how different situations present different problems and challenges to different people at different times in their lives no matter what your age or abilities!

Constance started Pilates with me at the Studio under protest as her daughter in law had bought her a course of six Pilates classes for a present. Constance had been in pain and diagnosed with osteoporosis and was advised to do some Pilates exercise. However, she was very apprehensive! Her skills and comfort zone were in the kitchen and she is a great cook, even teaching it in a school prior to her retirement. She came along and unenthusiastically joined a class. To her surprise Constance managed to keep up with the class doing all the exercises but didn't really enjoy it much. She did however, persevere with the classes for six weeks and started to see her muscles toning up and her strength returning. Her back was also hurting less. Constance made the decision that she would attend the Pilates classes with her best friend because "it was good for her". She would much rather have been cooking, gardening or doing her artwork. After a couple of months, I installed mirrors in the Studio all the way down one wall. Much to the surprise and horror of a few of my clients including Constance. They could all now see themselves from top to bottom! That day I found out that Constance really doesn't like mirrors! Now she even joins in the zoom classes and sees herself on camera. Constance is much more confident after participating in the Pilates classes improving her strength, mobility, and reducing the number of falls and bone breakages she was getting! (mainly a handful of wrist and arm fractures and breaks) She feels so much more confident and happier with herself after gaining strength and now she does enjoy coming along to class! One thing she never thought she would say!

To give you an example of how Pilates can not only prepare you for what might be some of the worst moments of your life, it can also help you to rebuild it afterwards. This is Beatrice's story.

Beatrice started Pilates classes at the school with me approximately 8 years ago. Her aim was mainly to destress from her demanding teaching job and resolve back and hip pain caused by a twisted pelvis. She wanted to improve her core strength and her Osteopath recommended Pilates classes. She had progressed to intermediate and advanced level Pilates exercises and was regularly coming along to class. Her pain had disappeared and she was feeling stronger happier and healthier. Beatrice has always been active regularly walking and has kept this up throughout her Pilates practice to ensure that she gets lots of fresh air and exercise to keep healthy. One day she found a lump in her breast which the doctors at the hospital thought was fatty tissue and was supposed to breakdown. After 18 months however it had got bigger and she went back to the doctors at the hospital to have it checked again. This time however a mammogram and MRI scan (with dye) they found cancer on her chest wall in the lobes and a secondary cancer where she had hurt her back originally when she first came to me. This came as a big shock to Beatrice and she had to have chemotherapy twice and radiotherapy and her breast removed to prevent the cancer from coming back. This has meant that the lymph nodes under her arm have been removed and her breast reconstructed from her tummy! Beatrice takes chemotherapy tablets to keep her cancer in her back under control as it could not be removed as it is on her spine. It was a very positive thing that she was fit prior to getting the cancer as she was able to have the 9 hour operation aiming to fix everything, rather than have to split the procedures.

Beatrice found recovery difficult as she was very tired, she was in pain in her chest area and under her arms where the lymph nodes were and her tummy was still healing up. She was struggling to dress herself and do basic tasks due to the pain and lack of movement. During this time Beatrice couldn't work as she worked as a teacher in the school. She had her operation in the June and didn't start back at work until Easter in the following year. She was planning to go back to work full time and had come up with a plan with her headteacher to do a phased return to school teaching with days off for hospital visits for the chemotherapy. She found that her headteacher was very supportive and understanding throughout her illness and the return to work. Beatrice found that she couldn't manage full time due to the extreme tiredness and fatigue she was still getting and agreed to work part time instead as she loved being a teacher at the school. Beatrice was getting very bored at home during the time she was ill and recovering made her emotions very unstable. She was suffering with anxiety and depression due to the breast and back cancer. Also, the grief and guilt of losing her Mum and Dad during her illness and recovery time, and not being able to look after them in the way that she would have liked.

This all meant that her confidence had hit rock bottom. Beatrice had very supportive friends who took her out walking initially and then persuaded her to come back to the Pilates class. I did a few 121 private sessions with her to figure out how much she could move and where the pain was. Beatrice surprised herself with how much movement she could actually do as she had a brand new tummy and breast and was unsure of her body's capabilities. Working together we created a simple plan that she could follow when she was at home or in a group class. Gradually Beatrice moved to the group class with her friend and loved the social aspect of exercising with other people. Regaining confidence in her own body and its capabilities after going through a lot with the cancer and the treatment. Her pain has reduced and the lymphatic drainage throughout her body has improved with the movement from Pilates and some of the stretches. She has improved her nutrition with good food and drinking lots of water making her feel a whole lot better. Beatrice's strength, flexibility and mobility has increased and is gradually returning to what it was prior to the operation. Pilates has improved her overall body image and confidence and she is now a lot happier and more energetic at work.

The above two case studies demonstrate how looking after yourself and keeping fit does a lot for your self esteem and confidence. Even if you think you may not be any good at it or are in a lot of pain. Attending a Pilates class makes you feel more confident and energised with your own body and should help with other areas of your life e.g. returning to a sport you enjoy or increasing your confidence at work! The Pilates classes can be taken as 121 private sessions or as a group dependant on your needs and requirements. The class will be tailored to you and your ability whether that is fast or slow! Why not try a class to see if it could help you?

I typically work with ladies from 35 to 45 years of age with back pain, who are passionate about having an active life, gain confidence, want to reduce their pain and return to their favourite sport.

Would you like to become pain free and increase your confidence by trying a Pilates class? The Pilates class can be at The Chatsworth Studio in Cheam Village or in your own home via Zoom or Skype.

If you are in pain a private 121 is advised as you would get more specialist attention and I can work out a specific programme for you to get the best out of your lessons and progress and become more confident.

To find out if we are a match and how I can help you why not try a FREE Private 121 class?

Mike Lawrence

Making people more confident

Mike's career began by improving the well-being of thousands of holidaymakers through positive engagement, reassurance and mindfulness. Mike wasn't aware at the time how valuable this knowledge and experience would become and how these skills would underpin and be pivotal to his well-being journey.

Mike has since progressed into offering a much more unique and personalised service as a well-being practitioner, which has brought him national and international acclaim and a constant stream of private and corporate clients.

After treating many hundreds of clients both here and abroad, and coaching thousands of company employees on motivation, confidence and mental well-being; the improved productivity, morale and motivation speaks for itself.

Now, with over 100 training lectures completed and speaking engagements on the topical issues of anxiety, stress and depression, the Mike Lawrence Clinic is gaining an excellent reputation. As well as being one of the top clinics in Sheffield it has earned robust local reviews and positive trading standards for trust, value and general excellence.

That's Mike Lawrence, his infectious smile, experience in life and sincerity guides many individuals to build their confidence to make successful and life-changing decisions in both their personal and professional lives.

Website: www.mikelawrence.co.uk

Email: mike@mikelawrence.co.uk

Phone: +44(0)1143 272 683

What If I Told You That I Was The First Black Redcoat In The UK, And On Arrival, I Was An Introvert And Low In Confidence?

As a young lad in my early 20s, I got the opportunity to go to Butlins in Bognor Regis about 250 miles away; I seized the opportunity with both hands.

At the end of the first season at Butlins, the Entertainments Manager invited me to a meeting, and I remember him saying how I had become increasingly confident and an important part of the team. He was keen that I return the following year to continue the excellent work and offered me a contract for the next season.

I returned to Butlins holiday centre following this with my two daughters and my ex-wife, and I remember taking them into the entertainments office and on the wall was a large photograph of all the Redcoats, and there I was amongst 40 or more staff.

I want to think that I paved the way for other black people in the UK; that they too could aspire to be a Redcoat.

Working in the leisure industry allowed me to participate in many activities, including football regularly.

Sadly, this came to an abrupt end when I ruptured my Achilles tendon, twice.

The Achilles tendon a tough band of fibrous tissue,

connects the calf muscles to the heel bone (calcaneus). It was the most significant injury that I'd suffered in my life.

In a consecutive injury, I ruptured my right leg in Barbados on the second day of the holiday.

I returned home where I heard about a Japanese therapy, to treat my Achilles tendon injury. This became the start of my practitioner journey. I joined a class of students to learn this art form, along with meditation, Qi Gong, Tai Chi and Yoga.

I continued with these enlightening lectures until I relocated back to Yorkshire to start a new job. This also coincided with the start of a divorce, which was one of the most difficult periods of my adult life. The proceedings took two years to settle at the cost of over £100k.

However, even in my darkest place, my newfound interest in well-being kept me going, and I felt my confidence was increasing.

All Endings are also beginnings; we just don't know it at the time' Mitch Albom.

This renewed belief gave me the confidence to raise some money as I began rebuilding my life and career. This eventually led me to open my health & well-being clinic in Sheffield. I know can help people using my life experience and professional techniques I have invested in to guide them through the most challenging times.

A client called Lucy came to see me, she is in her 40s, had gone through a divorce, has two young boys to her ex-husband, and she was only communicating with her ex-husband through her mum. When she initially came to see me, she had been signed off work for three months.

I remember the first couple of sessions she was extremely emotional; she felt alone. At work she was being supported by an Occupational Health specialist, she recounted, were not much help. Her GP merely prescribed anti-depressants and had neither the time nor the resources to get to the root cause of the problem.

She was also being bullied at work.

Lucy told me that she received no support, from her predominantly male colleagues and a boss who was indirectly blaming her for a task that didn't go to plan.

This may sound like a familiar scenario to many people.

When she first came to see me, I recognised that she had lost all her self-confidence, motivation and a sense of purpose owing to these events.

Over the ensuing months of therapy with me, she made significant progress; I set about understanding the root cause of her problem, by talking through the highs and lows in her childhood, her experience and memories of school—past relationships and career.

In Lucy's first session, I released some past emotional blockages which had put a stranglehold on her life. Following the release, she said, "I've got me back."

She decided not to return to her job but successfully negotiated a redundancy package, became a self-employed businesswoman and landed her first contract before she had even registered her business.

Now, Lucy says she is more in control of her life. Her

motivation and confidence levels have returned, and she has a bright future. Had Lucy not seen me, she says she would not have found her true self, and she would certainly not have had the confidence to make the changes and progress that she continues to enjoy in her life today.

Lucy's story is typical of the results from hundreds of clients that I have successfully helped in the last few years.

Vanessa shared with me recently how she changed her life 17 years ago, following coaching sessions with me.

After the conversation, they gave her more self-belief and confidence in relationships and friendships following the struggles with the loss of her identity, self-sabotaging patterns and unhappy childhood.

I met Katie at a wellness retreat in Sri Lanka, and during the week, she shared with me several problems she was experiencing in her work and life.

She was a senior manager; her employers had merged with a rival company, and she was struggling for many years with her mental health adapting to the new culture. It negatively affected her sleep patterns, relationships and confidence.

While in Sri Lanka, I was asked by the guests to host a mindfulness session. Katie attended this event. Following her return to the UK, she contacted me and said "OMG-Mike it's so lovely to hear your voice. You have been an amazing influence for me-like you would never believe." Our discussions individually and in the group sessions and my efforts to guide her into new thought paths convinced her to make drastic changes. She quit her job and is now retraining to be a schoolteacher.

Therefore, I decided to create an easy yet effective and powerful system that anyone suffering from a lack of confidence, motivation or resilience could immediately apply and benefit from when they work with me.

I help people to rediscover their identity, so they feel physically and mentally better equipped and in better control of their life.

Please contact me directly for more information on how this can work for you. Email enquiries@mikelawrence.co.uk or call 07967 052585.

"I've learned that people will forget what you said, people will forget what you did, but people will never forget how you made them feel." — Maya Angelou.

Jane McDowell

Bristol's Favourite Drug-free Migraine & Headache Solution

2019 winner of the Heart Centred Business Award for Outstanding Service, Jane has 20 years' experience of helping people get out of pain. Her work focuses on drug-free pain solutions primarily working with people suffering from debilitating migraines.

Jane's transformational work with migraine sufferers means that they see a significant reduction in the number of migraines they have and the intensity of the pain they experience. As a result, they regain their confidence, energy and focus so they flourish and succeed in their relationships and careers.

Website: www.drugfreemigrainesolutions.com

Email: jane@drugfreemigrainesolutions.com

Phone: +44(0)7779 023 117

The Pain/Confidence Connection

Have you ever noticed that people who are in constant or frequent pain are less likely to get excited when they receive an invitation to an event or are gifted an opportunity? Have you ever wondered why? The answer is that the physical pain they endure has dented their confidence, it's ground them down and slowly chipped away at their sense of enthusiasm and joie de vivre. Enthusiastic responses have been replaced by an underlying sense of dread. How come? Because for people living in pain their initial thought is most often, 'oh no, I bet I'll be in pain'.

Many migraine sufferers live in fear of the pain and disruption that migraines bring. They often feel guilty and embarrassed about constantly taking time off work, letting down their family and friends, feeling judged and talked about all of which affects their confidence in so many areas of their lives.

Imagine counting down the days to that holiday you've been looking forward to or to your best friend's wedding. Now imagine that instead of a growing sense of excitement you experience a growing sense of fear, the fear of being struck with an attack of pain. Imagine feeling your levels of anxiety increasing and your confidence in your ability to stay well diminishing the closer you got to the big day.

I know these reactions all too well because I suffered from frequent migraines for many years. I remember a friend gifting me tickets to see one of my favourite bands and she was taken aback that I wasn't jumping for joy. She thought she'd made a mistake and that I didn't like the band. Truth was I was incredibly grateful for her generous gift but my first thought was 'oh no, what if I have a migraine?' My mind instantly took me to the worst case scenario rather than revelling in the moment. I felt so bad that I didn't immediately express heartfelt thanks and joy at receiving the gift and I was left feeling that she thought I was an awful person.

It's incidents and feelings such as this that chip away at your confidence, when you start to believe that you're a bad friend, that you're flaky, unreliable, boring etc. and that even when you have times when you're not in pain you live in constant fear of pain returning. It's this constant underlying fear that robs you of the ability to live in the moment, to be present and enjoy the times when you're pain free.

Migraines made my life miserable and, aside from the pain, I felt judged all the time. My confidence really took a knock when I was referred to the occupational health team by my boss, I was convinced that he thought I was a liar and that he didn't trust me. I was a nervous wreck if I left my house without any migraine medication because I was terrified of having a migraine not only because of the pain and nausea but also because of the anxiety I felt about what others thought of me. Many of my clients share similar experiences.

When my client Isobel first came to me for help she was suffering 3 to 4 migraines a month and consequently having to take a lot of time off work. She'd landed her dream job a couple of months before and her sickness absence record was already giving her new employer cause for concern. Isobel was desperate for help as her life was being blighted by regular debilitating migraines. She was afraid she might lose her job, she believed that her work colleagues thought she was flaky and unreliable, she wasn't able to play netball and go to the gym as often as she wanted and she felt she was becoming unfit and unhealthy which in turn made her less body confident. She felt like she was letting down her family when she wasn't able to travel to see them at weekends and her friends when she would often have to duck out of social events at the last minute. She was fearful about the long-term prospects for her relationship with her partner as she wasn't spending much good quality time with them because she was so often hiding away in a darkened room unable to communicate. Her confidence was slowly but surely being chipped away by the pain and disruption that migraines were having on her life and she was struggling to see a bright future for herself either in her personal life or in her career.

In short, she was very unhappy and unconfident when she first came to see me. Thankfully all that changed, after the 1st treatment with me she didn't have another migraine for 6 months and 18 months later she'd only had 3 migraines. The effect of living without the constant fear of a migraine has transformed her confidence, even the way she holds herself is remarkably different, she has transformed from someone who was often in tears to someone who smiles and laughs with ease and is enjoying life once again. She now rarely takes time off work, she's feeling fit and healthy once again playing netball and going to the gym, her relationship with her partner is blossoming and she's enjoying spending time with family and friends, no longer feeling guilty about letting them down.

If your confidence levels have taken a bashing because of frequent pain or because you're living in fear of the next episode of pain then it's important to deal with the root cause. With migraines there are often more than one cause or trigger; it can be the combination of a number of factors. For instance, not getting enough sleep might not cause a migraine in and of itself. However, combine a lousy night's sleep on top of a stressful day when you haven't had time or opportunity to eat well and it can be the perfect recipe for a migraine.

If being in frequent or constant pain is affecting your ability to function how you'd like to and denting your confidence there is help at hand. Oftentimes when we go to see GPs we are given a prescription for pain killers and these are all well and good in the short run but in the long term they can have a detrimental effect on our health. We need to look for other ways of helping ourselves, there are so many ways to manage pain other than with over the counter or prescription drugs and crucially if you can identify and treat the cause of the pain the results are priceless.

It's my mission in life to help as many people as I can who suffer from migraines and headaches so that as well as being in less pain they get to regain the confidence they have lost from being in long-term or frequent pain. If this is something that affects you or someone in your world then help is at hand, simply pick up the phone or email me for a chat about how I might be able to help you and let's get you on the road to a more confident you.

Jane McDowell

Janemcdowell9@googlemail.com

07779 023117

Lisa Moore

No 1 Back Pain practitioner in Warwickshire

Lisa has been successfully treating back pain since 2001 with clients from all over the UK. Having delivered more than 100 lectures to companies and associations, Lisa has won the Leamington Business Award for Customer Excellence and was Runner Up in the best small business category. She held the contract for providing sports massage to the WWE wrestlers when touring the UK and provides massage at corporate and sporting events nationwide.

Lisa gets people moving again pain free. Are you interested in transforming your body so you can live your life again? If so, contact Lisa.

Website: www.leamingtontherapycentre.co.uk

Email: lisa@leamingtontherapycentre.co.uk

Phone: +44(0)1926 833 003

Lack Of Confidence Is Like Driving Through Life With Your Hand Brake On!

Nobody is born with limitless self confidence. Someone who seems that way has probably worked on it for years. It is something you can learn to build up through the challenges of work and life.

I'm treating more and more people with lack of confidence yet on assessing them, they are experiencing physical pain. The main reason for this is poor posture. This can be helped and prevented with knowledge, education and realignment of the body through treatment, strength training and rehabilitation.

Many years ago I was sitting in the corporate world at an office desk over a PC. My confidence and self worth was pretty low. I wasn't enjoying my job or the changes being made in my department. Panic attacks were frequent and I was always tired and constantly yawning. I felt 'burnt out'. I would admire the incredibly confident people I met and would notice one thing they all had in common, an upright and relaxed posture, which in turn portrayed confidence. I would ask myself, '...How do you get a posture like that?'

I'd developed an interest in health, wellness and the human body (which led me to my career change a few years later) and was reading an article about habits, behaviour and muscle memory. Did you know it takes an average of 66 days for a new behaviour to become automatic? Great I thought to myself, I'm going to start with my first wish, to be able to sit down without crossing my legs. I put a post-it note on my computer screen which read 'uncross legs'. Whenever I crossed my legs I'd see this and uncross them. It wasn't too long before this became habit. Soon after I was implementing others in the same manner to help me improve my posture and before long I noticed a dramatic improvement with my confidence. I was breathing better and I was calmer. Still the unhappiness in my career was slowly eating away at me physically, mentally and emotionally. Finally I decided to take the plunge and do a course that would lead me to my desired career. Now I have my own thriving business in Leamington Spa with associates working from my clinic. We help others become more confident, energising and revitalising themselves and teaching them how they can correct most of it.

This generation has a seen a big shift in work practice with an increased use of technology and hours spent in a car travelling long distances. People strive to meet deadlines, targets and achieve promotion. The modern person juggling work and family life putting themselves under pressure to do it all perfectly. In turn these lifestyle changes have altered us making us believe we are inadequate.

The effects of good posture:

- More confidence in your thoughts,
- Puts you in charge of making your own decisions,
- Creates a positive mood,
- Better overall health,
- Less impact on the physical body which in turn has

less impact on your mental state,

- More confident choices.

Your posture reflects your behavior, is something I always tell my clients. When you stand or sit up tall, and pull your shoulders back and down, your brain gets a signal that it's the confident, powerful you in charge. In turn you'll feel more confident. It also has a huge impact on your mental and physical health.

Good body posture indicates that you are confident, have respect for yourself and those in your company. Client A came to see me after experiencing panic attacks and low self esteem. Her confidence hit rock bottom after she was unsuccessful in a job promotion. She was in chronic pain in her upper back which she had endured for months, having migraines on a daily basis. She was in a high powered job sitting at a desk all day and was finding it difficult to concentrate. Her productivity had reduced and she was afraid of not reaching her targets. More to the point afraid of not providing for her family.

Her lack of confidence had changed her posture and this was causing physical stress. In turn the pain from this physical stress was causing her mental stress. Her high workload was creating more mental stress and because she was sitting for long periods of time she suffered more physical stress. All of which made her lack confidence. Her back was so painful to touch that the first session was just to introduce her muscles to the changes they were about to go through.

With an exercise plan in place, advice on diet, sleep and how to set up her workstation she noticed a big difference after just one treatment. Still a long way to go we went on a journey together increasing her confidence, her self worth, eliminating the muscular pain, realigning and strengthening her posture and educating her on the things she could do to help herself. Within a short period of time we had eradicated all of her symptoms and she was back feeling more positive about herself, enjoying her work and family life again with more confidence.

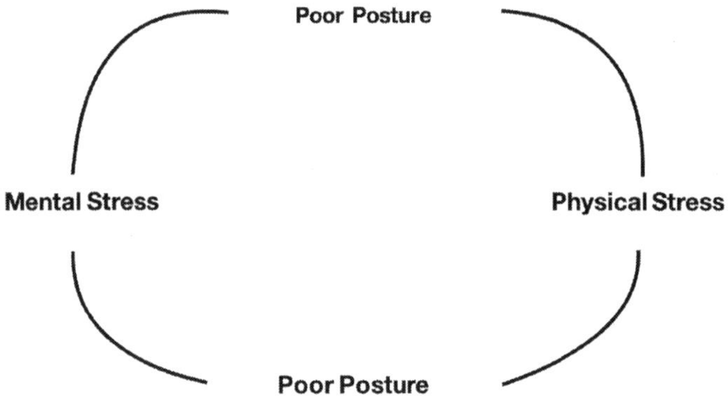

5 Top tips to increase your confidence.

- Remember to ask yourself throughout the day 'How am I sitting/standing?' Stand or sit tall with your shoulders back and down and your head held high,
- Get moving, keep fit with cardio & strength and rebalance with yoga or pilates, exercise increases the endorphins in the brain making you feel more positive,
- Eat the right food, foods high in sugar will cause mood spikes and crashes,

- Stay hydrated with water,
- Have regular maintenance massage, it's a great way to make you feel better.

After years of experiencing lack of confidence and self worth I met Lisa has been working her magic on me for the last 4 weeks. My confidence has grown and my muscular pain has greatly reduced from the first session. I feel very confident in Lisa's skills and I'm very grateful we crossed paths. I highly recommend a visit to Lisa.

Liz Wood

After two appointments with Lisa my posture had greatly improved and my movement is now 100% better. I am holding myself better and look more confident than ever before. I would strongly recommend anyone see Lisa as she is extremely thorough and effective with her results.

John Wills

Irma Prins

Helping kids move freely

Irma has been unlocking people's energy by helping them to move the way they are designed to for 3 decades now. When she started applying her physiotherapy skills to young children, whilst they were positioned on a walking horse (hippotherapy/ equine facilitated physiotherapy), she was amazed about how much progress they made in their development and how quickly they achieved it. Since then she has been keen to see as many children benefit from this as possible.

Therefore, she has helped shape the future of hippotherapy/ equine facilitated therapy and the education of therapists through her roles in the committee of the Chartered Physiotherapists in Therapeutic Riding and Hippotherapy (CPTRH), UK. She has served on this Specialist Interest Group for 8 years. She also took part in the first European Equine Facilitated Therapy Network meeting in Prague in 2019, where decisions were made about the definition of Equine Facilitated Therapy, and a plan was developed on how to bring all the expertise in Europe together under one umbrella. Irma runs lectures for other professionals.

Irma is based in the Midlands, UK and expanding! Out of area? Don't worry. Sessions without horses can be done on-line.

Email: irma@irmaprins.com

Facebook: FreedomPhysioServices

Phone: +44(0)7402 825 904

What If I Told You That Positioning Children Well, Gives Them Confidence And Independence?

Would you like to know how 2 year old children, who struggle to develop their motor skills, such as lying on their tummy, sitting, standing or walking, increase their confidence and gain their independence using my 3 step system? In this chapter I will show you how.

For almost 3 decades I've worked with people with brain injuries. I have seen the effect this can have on people emotionally as well as physically. Unable to trust their own bodies to perform, can, especially, make children feel they don't fit in. It can stop them from doing the things they would love, like playing with their friends. I help them to achieve the right posture for an activity, so they can move freely and with confidence.

Through my training and experiences I have developed a 3 step system. Step 1 is to find out what is stopping the person from achieving the right posture for the movement he or she wants to do, and to solve this. This could be tightness or weakness. Step 2 is to practice the posture while moving. Step 3 is to make it even harder by adding more challenges so the new skill becomes automatic. I applied this system to my own movement problems when I wanted to improve my horse riding skills. It really helped me to feel safe and confident, because I was no longer bouncing up and down like a bag of potatoes.

I would love to tell you some stories about how I have used this 3 step system with young children on horse back, because typically that works even quicker and better! There are some elements that being on horse back adds to the equation, such as fun, stimulation of all the senses, and a set of unique repetitive movements, which all contribute to the learning of a new skill and can't be replicated to the same extent in clinic. *Of course, using horses in therapy is a skill which needs to be learned by trained professionals. It also requires a dedicated trained team of assistants to keep the child safe and special horses which are selected for their temperament and for their movements.*

The first story is about 2 year old Lily.

Lily was born 5 weeks early and she spent a lot of time in hospital due to health issues. She wasn't able to develop normally in this time, which meant that she learned all her movements in a slightly different way. Her back muscles were much stronger than her tummy muscles, so she tended to use these instead of her tummy and legs (step 1- identifying the cause, in this case weak tummy and leg muscles). This abnormal way of moving meant that she was struggling to stand by herself and let go of support to take steps on her own. This is when I was called in.

Firstly, I set up a programme with her parents and the nursery staff to help her gain more control over her tummy muscles (resolving the identified cause of non-alignment to complete step 1). She then practised that control in all the positions she used for playing (step 2). We also taught her how to use her legs for standing up etcetera. Everyone worked brilliantly with her so results came straight away.

This is something you can do with your child at home: make sure your child is always positioned well in their everyday activities. This might mean a verbal correction or a gentle touch to help them achieve this. It could be placing toys just in the right place or it could be that they need support in the form of special equipment.

We then went to the riding centre and, after introducing Lily to the pony, we placed her on top in the right position facing the tail end (step 1). We then asked the pony to walk (step 2). This movement would gently push her off balance encouraging her to use her tummy muscles to steady herself. Due to the many repetitions of the movements, her muscles became stronger and stronger. When she could keep her balance facing backwards, we moved her into a forward facing position on the pony. This was more challenging for Lily (step 3).

When Lily started working on the horse, her improvement at home accelerated and she felt increasingly more confident. After a few weeks her mum reported that Lily was walking around by herself.

The second story is about Jimmy, a 14 month old boy with Down's syndrome. He was unable to lift his head up while on his tummy, so when asked, he just rolled himself onto his back again. He needed full support to sit up. He enjoyed lying on his front on the pony, and after only 4 sessions he had gained enough energy to steady his head better at home. He could now bring his fingers up to his mouth: the start of eating interdependently! He was so confident in his sitting abilities that he didn't need his bath seat anymore. He could now enjoy the water much more freely.

Finally, I like to tell you the story of Jacob. Jacob was in a car accident when he was still a small baby, causing injury to his brain. This resulted in weakness in all 4 of his limbs, especially his right arm and leg. He had difficulties keeping his balance when placed in a sitting position on the floor, so he had to be supervised to keep him safe. His therapist asked me if I could see him on the horse, so I could help him to learn to control his upper body and pelvis because this is so important for developing good balance in all positions and movements.

After trying different treatment methods, we decided that the most effective approach was with me sitting behind him on the horse while stabilising his pelvis in the right position (step 1). The horse's movement in walk really challenged his balance (step 2) and following a few weekly sessions his body became so strong that he was confident enough to sit independently and play with a toy in front of him on the floor. Over the months, less support was needed when working on the horse (step 3) and half a year after starting, Jacob felt safe enough at home to pull himself up into standing whenever he had the chance. After another half a year he was able to sit by himself on the pony and at home he had the confidence to walk, while holding onto furniture or someone's hands.

The above are examples of how children gained their confidence and became more independent by using the 3 step system. Are you curious about how this could help your son or daughter? If so, then please email me on irma@irmaprins.com or phone +44 7402 825904 so we can schedule a 1 hour consultation and find out how we can work together to help your child gain the confidence he/ she is looking for. Sessions without horses are also available on-line.

Simon Rogers

The Feel Better Coach

Simon has worked with thousands of clients across Europe for over 15 years. He has helped them solve long-standing stress-related upper back and neck pain leading them to live more successful and fulfilling lives.

He's found that working with people as people, physically, emotional and mentally rather than focusing only on their symptoms allows them to work at the root cause. This provides them with not only a lasting solution to their pain but means that they can fall in love with a life that they are now consciously creating.

What would you be able to do if you were able to solve your pain for good?

Website: www.restoreyourbodynow.co.uk

Email: simon@restoreyourbodynow.co.uk

Phone: +44(0)2083 966 668

Growing Your Unshakable Confidence

When you hear a baby screaming at the top of its lungs on a packed airplane, does it lack confidence? When a baby falls again and again when attempting to crawl, stand or walk does it lack confidence? Never! This is how we all start out and yet we still end up reading a book about confidence later in our lives. How did we get here?

Self-confidence is a belief in oneself, the conviction that one has the ability to meet life's challenges and to succeed. In my experience there are two players in self-belief, and they are love and fear. And what is the biggest challenge connecting both? Perfectionism!

Perfectionism was my biggest challenge growing up. To me perfectionism is a compensation to a fear of believing that you are not enough. I wasn't conscious of this as a young boy, I just always felt a huge drive to do my best at everything I did. There was nothing wrong with this drive, it helped me achieve a lot; become a talented young football player, go to leading local school, graduate from university in the Netherlands, become a lecturer, become fluent in Dutch despite dyslexia, graduate again with a second degree, start and develop my own business to help thousands of clients to overcome their physical and emotional challenges. Because my drive was from fear the achievements ultimately felt hollow; they never felt enough because I never believed that I was enough. Is this something you can relate to?

An important ingredient was added to my life and it's called grief. It's not something you can tough out no matter how hard you try. If you do, it starts to fester at the very core of you and strengthen the belief that you are not enough. I know this because this is exactly what I did and what I've seen happen many, many times.

Growing up my best friend was my Grandad. I didn't want to show any of my insecurities to anyone else because I felt like I needed to be example to everyone else around me. We shared a passion for football, and he would be at every match I played. Sometimes I would play 3-4 times per week and he would travel for hours just comes watch my games. I could level with him about how was feeling and it would never affect his unshakable belief in me as a football player and most importantly as a person. I loved him very much.

When I was about 10 years old, I was told by my parent that he was diagnosed with colon cancer. To be honest, as most 10-year olds, I didn't have a clue what this meant, and I didn't ask. I just knew that it meant that he was having an operation and that if he ever needed the toilet, he would have to get there quicker than usual now. He still had his characteristically infectious enthusiasm for life about him so nothing had changed as far as I could see. When I was 17 years old, he become increasingly ill. I was in complete denial that he was going to die. I remember my mum asking me if I would like to go and see him. My entire family went, and I stayed behind. That was the last time I would have seen him alive. I just remember feeling numb and beneath this was a deep sadness but also a painful guilt. The story I told myself was that after all the support that my grandad had given me, I wasn't there for him when he needed me the most. This story was eating away at me and gave me a can of petrol to douse the fire inside me that was already blazing. The flames would hiss and whisper to me that I was never going to be worthy of love and this was why!

The only approach I used to deal with this was to tough it out. I wouldn't speak with anyone about it. I felt so ashamed and I couldn't risk sharing this with anyone. If I shared it and they validated that indeed I should feel ashamed, I didn't know if I could live with that.

The feeling of not being enough was so clear that I was sure that everyone else could feel it whenever they would come near me. I could feel it throbbing in my body as my brain went all fuzzy, my chest tight, my breathing shallow and mostly there was a big gaping whole where my heart should have been. I just couldn't let anyone near me. I got better and better at hiding it. I couldn't let anyone in and then be rejected. I didn't know if I was able or willing to survive that.

But I was desperate for love. The problem was that due to my intense belief that I wasn't worthy of love, I thought I had to be so much more than myself to have a chance of someone loving me. A few short-lived romance dramas played out and decided it was safer to put my efforts into doing my very best for my clients. Even though, all my clients would come to me to help them to resolve their physical pain somehow, I was often able to connect with them about an emotional pain. Then just by listening to them and not passing any judgement, even in my head, they would share guilt and shame that they had been carrying for years. They described feeling lighter inside. I admired their courage deeply and longed to feel this way too.

Gradually, I started to let people closer to me and my trust started to build. As my trust grew with my friends, I gave myself permission to share my story of letting my grandad down and to my surprise, I wasn't judged, I felt a wave of emotion release out of me as it flowed out from my chest, through my throat and out the top of my head. I hysterically sobbed for a few minutes and when it passed, I felt lighter. So much lighter!

Letting my wife into my life has strengthened my confidence in letting go of what I'm not. I can feel that she loves me for me and not who I think I need to be. This will be a journey that I'm on for this rest of my life and I'm now confident that I'm headed in the right direction.

Why have I shared my story with you now? Because I want you to learn quicker than I did that the foundation of confidence is belief in yourself. I've found that this belief often doesn't have a chance to truly grow if you are carrying fear. It poisons the soil, and nothing can grow. You have to clear these stories out. Once they are gone you get to know yourself and have a steady foundation to build your confidence. A confidence that is based on the truth: That you are worthy of love.

If you are curious about what is possible for you or loved one, then I have a special gift for you. If you send 'Uncovering the confident me' to hello@restoreyourbodynow.co.uk then I will send you a complimentary video series to get you started on your journey.

David Roylance

Helping Women to Shine When They Speak and Giving Them The Opportunity To Make 10 Times The Difference.

With over 25 years of experience in the world of coaching and development, David is a Leading Voice Specialist, having coached 100+ women in how to achieve promotion and an extra £100k+ in their income stream.

Prior to this David had a prestigious career in the theatre, first as an actor and then as a director and producer for this own theatre company. David has presented to 1000+ through Europe, Africa, India and the US, owner of 6 figure business, trained sales teams to achieve £50 to £100k growth in their individual turnover.

He connects people to the powerful voice they don't yet know they possess, forcing those above them in the management chain to recalibrate and promote up to the board.

Website: www.davidroylance.com

Email: david@davidroylance.com

Phone: +44(0)2087 206 834

If Barack Obama Can Be President, So Can You!

There was a time when former President of the United States Barack Obama was considered to be someone without presence or the charisma necessary to sway large groups of people.

With regards to the title of this chapter, I understand that there are some rules about who can stand for President of the United States. Let's pretend that those rules didn't exist. If the world were like that, then my title stands.

If he can, anyone can.

How do I know this?

I am David Roylance and professionally I dedicate my life to helping people shine in whatever they do so that they can deliver 10 times more energy to their role through newly achieved confidence. My greatest successes with clients have been helping senior women within the corporate world who, when they first come to me, feel that they have no voice and therefore no confidence. The women I work with typically put an extra 100k or more into their income streams as a result of their new found confidence.

Might you be reading this because you would like create something similar?

Perhaps you might like to hear about my client who has created an extra £300k in her income stream through 2 internal promotions and being head hunted by a competitor.

Perhaps you might like to hear about my public sector client who had a visit from her bosses offering to create a new role specifically to fit the remit she wanted to occupy, and with a pay band upgrade on top.

In order to help you understand how I help my clients achieve these amazing results, let me tell you my story.

I am a professionally trained actor. I went to Guildhall School of Music and Drama in London back in the early 1990s. Guildhall is considered one of the top 3 conservatoire trainings for actors in the world. If my alumni of Daniel Craig, Ewen McGregor and Damien Lewis are anything to go by, I think it is safe to say that was true.

I trained with Patsy Rodenburg, the world's no 1 voice coach, for 3 years to use my voice as an actor. What she gave me in that time has served me phenomenally as a way to conquer my own lack of confidence and use that to help hundreds of corporate women every year to shine more brightly than ever before.

After leaving college I created my own theatre company. I directed and acted in a number of plays. I directed for theatre in education for many years. The most money I made as an actor was in presenting on behalf of corporates at conferences. It was a natural progression to start teaching their own sales people how to represent their company confidently with clarity. It was only when I was working with those people that I began to see the real value I could bring to the world.

I remember meeting Patsy Rodenburg in Heathrow airport about 12 years ago. I was on my way to do a theatre directing job in Germany and she was on the way to the US. The Democratic Party had called her and asked for her help. They had a potential presidential candidate who "had no charisma, had no presence", who lacked the confidence to inspire large groups. That candidate was Senator Barack Obama.

Which brings us back to the title of this chapter.

There is something that Barack Obama and Bill Clinton share, beyond having been President of the United States. When they were at University they were both told by tutors that "Whatever you do in life, don't do anything involving any kind of public speaking! You're terrible".

Public speaking we know to the world's no 1 fear. When we encounter fear we typically display to others the behaviours of anxiety. People see and hear lack of confidence.

When Barack Obama decided he wanted a certain job enough to work on this problem, then he invested in the solution that allowed him the space to change the world through his words.

That is why I say, if Barack Obama can, so can you. All you need is to know clearly what it is you want in order to decide if you want it enough to try something new and perhaps left-field, like the exercise I am sharing with you here.

This exercise transformed my life when I first started practising it, and has transformed the lives of several of my clients. Do this for 4 to 6 weeks, once a day, and within a month people will respond to you differently.

This is the 3 circles.

There are 3 different circles of energy in the way with communicate with others.

The 1st circle is the introvert state. It is the place we go to when we desire a conversation with ourselves. When we retreat into this internally focused state we mainly pull our energy back and carry our weight on the heel of the foot or against the back of a chair carry it if we are sitting. This is the flight aspect of fight or flight.

The 3rd circle is the other extreme. To call it an extravert state would be doing it a disservice. It is the convincing state. This is where we go when we wish to convince other people of something and display the behaviours of confidence without being confident. When standing we might carry our weight over the toes and when sitting we might lean into a table towards the people we wish to convince.

Although 1st and 3rd circle may be reflected to the world differently, internally they are exactly the same experience. They are both a form of anxiety. The posture and behaviour denotes lack of confidence. In both cases, you would be breathing in the chest. Your heart rate will be up and the heart will have sent signals to your brain which deprives the frontal lobe, where all your clever thinking happens, of oxygen.

Right in the centre of this is 2nd circle. 2nd circle is the state of balance, the only state where others can ascribe presence and confidence. It is both external and internal confidence.

You will know you are in 2nd circle because you are breathing deep into the stomach rather than the chest. For this to happen you either have to carrying your weight centrally in the foot. In fact the optimum would be slightly forward of centre, slightly on the ball of the foot. In a sitting position you would need to have your bottom at the front of a chair, both feet planted firmly on the ground and using your hips as a pivot swaying until you feel the breathe drop.

This is what I would ask you to do to find your 2nd circle.

Find a comfortable spot in a room to stand. Close your eyes and then come up onto your toes. From there, keeping you eyes closed, rock through the feet so you are swaying front and back. Keep this up for about 60 seconds. We deprive sight so the other senses can come to life and help you find balance.

After 60 seconds come back to standing. Keep your eyes closed and feel the moment your breath drops into the stomach. Then place your head where you believe directly ahead of you to be. Ask yourself this. Is the eyeline I have now higher or lower than the eyeline I hold in everyday life. If higher it suggests 1st circle is your stress default. If lower, 3rd circle.

If you want to be seen and heard as more confident, and feel it in yourself, do this exercise every day for 6 weeks. I guarantee others will notice a difference in you, and then you will feel it too.

I particularly remember my client, a female entrepreneur who ran a highly successful telecoms company and wanted to create her own personal brand from presenting, telling me what a revelation it was to her to realise that she had spent the majority of her life in 1st circle and that discovering 2nd circle had changed everything. Within 3 months she was debating government ministers during an election campaign and winning.

I am on a mission to help transform the lives of at least 1000 women by connecting them to the powerful, resonant voice they already possess and that they use it to achieve the kind of results I described in the paragraph above. I want to help at least 1000 women every year. That doesn't mean 1000 clients. It means I want the message to reach 1000 women.

Has this chapter made you curious? Would you like to find out more about how my clients fortunes change when they engage with our work? If the answer to those 2 questions are yes, then I have a gift for you. I have an ebook that goes into more detail than I can in this chapter. "Finding Your Personal Power". If you are curious and would like to take action with that curiosity, then email me at the address below and ask for the book and I will send it to you as a gift.

david@davidroylance.com

Sophie Thwaites

Helping children get back into their body and ready to learn

Sophie has helped children all over the world, with varying learning differences. She typically works with children, aged between 8-12 years old, who are struggling to read, write, sit still and coordinate their body.

She helps to find the source of their challenges and permanently reduce them through the use of movement-based exercises. Sophie has developed a broad understanding on how best to work with children, and how to help them establish greater connections with their surrounding environment.

Sophie has personal experience of the struggles and challenges school life can have on a child, and has a great passion to minimise this and to help other children reach their full potential.

Website: www.sophiethwaites.co.uk

Email: info@sophiethwaites.co.uk

Phone: +44(0)7584 857 861

Increasing Confidence In Children By Building A Stronger Foundation

The importance of confidence in children cannot be over-estimated. Confidence and self-esteem are the foundations on which a healthy life can be built, and often heavily relies on a child's belief in his or her own abilities. Children need to be aware of their own skills and feel like they are able to achieve. Many children find this hugely challenging; but through the combination of correct mentoring, education and therapy, children can begin to overcome some of their struggles, start to trust their abilities and grow in confidence.

However, the level of confidence our children have, does not always stem from their abilities, but to the connections created in their brain. The first few years of a child's life (starting from conception) play a vital role in creating and establishing a solid foundation for further development. Essential brain pathways are created during these first few years, but if not correctly formed at the right time or in the right order, can significantly impact a child's development. This can lead to later challenges around how they learn, how they co-ordinate their body, how they interact with their environment and how shy, anxious or confident they are.

Does this sound familiar? Does this sound like your child? Were there complications during pregnancy and/or birth? Was your child delayed in one or more of their developmental milestones within their first year of life? If you have answered yes to one or more of these, don't worry. There is a solution.

If, for any reason, these brain and body connections are not made during this period, we can actually create them later in life through specific movement programmes, ensuring that the child develops these strong foundations - crucial for all areas of life. Before I briefly cover the theory behind this, let me first start with my story.

When I was sixteen I moved to a new boarding school and it was the first time I was living away from my family. This new school was significantly larger than my previous one, with bigger classes, greater competition amongst pupils and less available support. I had always enjoyed my time in my previous school and was one of the top achieving pupils in the class. If school work was ever a challenge, there were always teachers on hand to offer guidance and support. However, moving to the larger school, I felt weighed down with the pressures of school work. The average level of intelligence had suddenly increased and the amount of support I received from teachers was reduced. My confidence took a significant knock, affecting my work and friendships. I was no longer the bubbly, confident child I had been. Instead I became reclusive and wanted to shy away from the world.

Within the first year of being at my new school, I was diagnosed with dyspraxia and dyslexia and was offered additional support. I received help with my essay writing, was taught tools to help me understand and retain information, and was provided with colour overlays to ease reading. But I didn't feel like these were helping, and instead felt like the gap between me and my peers was widening.

Fortunately, a staff member at the school had recently completed some training, which focused on movement-based exercises to help children overcome a range of challenges, including writing, co-ordination and concentration – my key difficulties. She assessed my suitability to the programme and I was soon set up on a 12-month programme. I was required to do a specific set of exercises, which mirrored early movements carried out as a baby, for 5-10 minutes every day, which changed every few weeks.

The changes I experienced over the course of the year were gradual; but after my family and I compared who I was before the 12 months to after, we realised the changes were astonishing. My grades had improved, my handwriting was a lot neater, my ability to concentrate and retain information was better, and my general co-ordination and balance had improved. But what was by far the greatest improvement was my confidence. Within the space of 12 months, I went from being a very shy, introverted girl, lacking confidence in both my academic abilities and who I was as a person, to becoming far more confident and grounded in all areas of life. So much so that I bought a plane ticket to go travelling on my own – something that would have filled me with crippling fear a few months earlier. But with my rediscovered confidence in my abilities and a new sense of calm, I felt excited about it rather than fearing it.

The programme that was so instrumental in shaping me into the person I am today, is the same one that I now use to help children overcome their challenges and reach their true potential. I have witnessed some incredible transformations in children over the years; and have seen huge improvements in areas such as writing, reading and maths, all without picking up a single pencil or book during the exercises.

The theory behind these transformational exercises lies with primitive reflexes. Primitive reflexes are a group of motor reflexes found in new-born babies. These develop within the womb and are essential in the birthing process, as they help the new-born take its first breath and support its early survival. They instinctively enable us to perform certain tasks such as feeding, grasping, responding to danger, listing our head, rolling, crawling, standing and eventually walking.

All being well, the primitive reflexes should be fully inhibited and integrated within the body, by the age of 1. If these reflexes are not suppressed in the first year, they can interfere with subsequent motor development, visual functioning (needed for reading), hand-eye co-ordination (needed for writing), and perceptual skills.

While there can be many social and educational factors for specific learning difficulties, physical abilities underpin every aspect of learning and social interaction. When these challenges are corrected, children can start to not only achieve, but thrive.

If these foundations are not strong enough when initially formed, even though the child may seem to be interacting with their environment adequately, when they encounter a new challenge they can be knocked off balance and underlying issues can start to display themselves. I believe this is what happened to me. By moving to a new school, where I suddenly felt out of depth, my foundations began to crack. I saw a decrease in my academic ability, felt less grounded, my relationships suffered, and my confidence took a knock.

Over the years I have witnessed incredible transformations and long-lasting changes in every child I have worked with; including confidence growth, improved writing, easier reading, and better co-ordination. The programme is simple, yet amazingly powerful. It works from the source of the challenges, creating a more solid foundation, from which everything else falls into place.

Exclusive Offer:

To receive your FREE e-booklet of simple, fun movement-based exercises, to help your child get back into their body and ready to learn (worth £99), contact me today. These will help to strengthen the connections between their brain and body – ultimately expanding their learning capabilities, improve relationships, interact with their environment with greater ease, and increase their overall confidence.

Phone: +447584857861

Email: info@sophiethwaites.co.uk

If you are curious to learn more about the bespoke programmes I run and how they could help your child on a much deeper level for long-lasting changes, please feel free to contact me or visit my website: www.sophiethwaites.co.uk

Bonus Chapter

Building Confidence By Focusing On The One Area Most People Avoid!

There's been so many great techniques, strategies and suggestions outlined by the authors of this book that I know you're already feeling a big shift in your confidence.

Or, perhaps at the very least, you're feeling more confident that you now have the tools to help yourself build your confidence and move your life forward in new ways. Please remember if you want any extra support, you can reach out to any of the authors in this book and explore what further support or advice they might be able to give you.

This final chapter is going to cover building confidence in a completely different way. And at first, what I'm about to discuss with you might seem somewhat left-field. In fact, some of you reading this are going to instantly switch off or get irritated and that's ok. Because the fact that you've been triggered or irritated by the topic we're about to cover, means you're ready to make some changes in this area, which in turn will increase your self-belief and give a massive boost to your confidence.

And what is this much neglected area that will have a profound impact on your confidence?

Money!

More specifically, the state of your finances and the impact this is having on your life.

I'm going to tell you the summary now....

If you want to increase your confidence, improve your financial security.

It's that simple! Yet when it comes to money, we are often so emotionally hung up by money that we put our head in the sand and ignore it. And yet a lack of money is perhaps one of the most damaging things you can do to yourself long term.

Now stay with me. Remember, I said that some of you might instantly be turned off by even the thought of money. However, money is a bigger deal than any of us typically admit. For example, financial worries are the number one reason cited for divorce! How crazy is that?! Just think about it.....two people love each other enough to commit to spending the rest of their lives together. Yet a lack of money can destroy this love and the relationship entirely?!

Many people say, "Money isn't important." And unfortunately, they are totally and damagingly wrong!

As the late great Zig Ziglar used to say, "Money is not the most important thing in life, but it is right up there just below oxygen." In today's society, we need money to do pretty much anything. You want to something eat, or a roof over your head, or clothes to wear? Either you pay for these things using your own money, or you have to accept charity from someone else who has the money to pay for them.

Not having enough money is incredibly stressful and knocks your self-belief. It will massively erode your confidence of being able to cope with whatever life throws at you.

If you're always worrying about paying your bills; or having enough money in your account to cover groceries; or paying for your children's education; these concerns will erode your sense of worth and happiness in the present moment. Unsurprisingly, your confidence then takes a hit. And it will keep on taking hits the longer that money concerns continue.

How do I know this?

I was once over £100,000 in debt.

And I was only earning around £20,000 a year.

So I know first-hand the impact a lack of money has!

Now I wish I could say that I was so badly in debt because of a crazy weekend in Las Vegas. Or perhaps that I was a victim of circumstances....."It wasn't my fault!" However, the reality is that I created this mess all on my own.

Yes, there were external factors. Yes, life threw me several curve balls. Yes, I come from a background and a family where we didn't have much money. However, fundamentally there are two factors that contributed to my financial reality and both are entirely and have always been under my control: my money mindset and my financial habits.

Working hard for money and not having much to go around was a large part of my family's unconscious mindset around money. The beliefs and mindsets we grow up with, that our parents have, are usually the beliefs we adopt as our own. Even when I had grown up and left home, I continued this pattern: I worked hard and put in the hours, yet always seemed to be struggling financially. This continued even when I started working as an Osteopath and earning what felt like a good income. Over time, things kept 'happening' to my money and whether I had a good month or a bad month, somehow, the money would disappear from my account. Somehow and someway, the money was always spent. It wasn't that anyone else was spending it, but my own unconscious habits and actions meant I was getting rid of my money, always spending more than I had, earning less than I wanted, and feeling smaller and smaller every month.

Now, why would I keep sabotaging myself and creating financial hardship when I was trying so hard to make money? It's because my unconscious brain was trying to give me a benefit it perceived as more important than my financial success: connection to my family. By continuing the pattern of not having enough money and working excessively hard I remained able to connect and relate in the same way I'd always done with my family. Entirely unconscious and unspoken, yet a fear of being different to my family meant I self-sabotaged my own finances and created a whole world of unnecessary debt, health-impacting stress and massive self-doubt.

It took me to being over £100,000 in debt and becoming a father before I finally made a commitment to do things differently and create a different reality. It definitely wasn't easy and it didn't happen overnight. However, changing my money mindset and my financial habits progressively over the past 7 years, my family and I are now financially secure for the rest of our lives, whether

I work or not. And much more importantly, my self-belief and confidence have sky-rocketed.

Is it having more money that increased my confidence?

No!

It's the knowledge and self-belief that no matter what happens in life I am able to make more money and look after my loved ones. Having more money in your bank account makes life easier. Whereas, being able to create more money gives you freedom and stops you being a victim of circumstances. This is where true confidence comes from!

So, let's explore the concepts of Money Mindset and Financial Habits more closely and look at what you can do to improve these areas in your own life.

The reality is that most people, like me, have poor Money Mindsets and poor Financial Habits.

Now in case my use of the word 'poor' has ruffled any feathers, let me explain what I mean...

Poor in this case can be translated as negative or detrimental. When it comes to the topic of money, negative or detrimental mindsets or habits will lead to a poor financial reality, meaning a very real lack of money. So saying a poor Money Mindset and poor Financial Habits is true in all senses.

And of course, I know that some people will read this and say something like, "But it's not my fault, I was raised poor", or, "My family has never had any money so I never had a chance", or "No one has money where I'm from", or, "Who is he to judge me as poor, just because he has lots of money?"

Remember, what we think internally about money, our mindset is part of what creates our reality. If you're feeling any negative reaction to my using the word 'poor', this is great as you're getting a useful insight into something that might be holding back your finances and therefore your confidence and ease of life. And remember, I was over £100,000 in debt before I started realising this stuff for myself and taking steps to change things. Hopefully you're nowhere near my position so your journey will be a lot easier than mine was!

Money Mindset:

Whatever you're currently experiencing with money, you have created it for yourself. Now I understand that some of you have just thrown your arms up in disgust saying something along the lines of, "It's not my fault that I have no money! He/she/they/it did this to me..." I totally agree that life and circumstances happen to all of us....bad relationships, losing jobs, cars breaking down, the boiler blowing up or any other unexpected expense...there are many ways that life can throw financial challenges at us. It is how we respond to those challenges that determines how much money we have.

This is what I meant earlier when I said my confidence comes from no longer being a victim of circumstances. Life will always happen, yet we always have the choice of how we respond. It's our Money Mindset that largely determines our response.

Consider what phrases or beliefs you might have in your mind around the concept of money...?

Money doesn't grow on trees

Money is the root of all evil

Money is dirty

Greedy people are evil

Rich people have destroyed the world

Do you think having any of these beliefs would lead to a positive relationship with money?

And do you think someone having these beliefs would be happy to bring more money into their life? Of course not! For example, anyone believing that rich people are destroying the world will unconsciously do anything to prevent themselves from becoming rich otherwise they'll feel they're to blame for what's going wrong with the world right now.

A poor or negative Money Mindset will lead to poor or detrimental financial habits, such as over-spending, a poor work ethic, bad investments or a myriad of other self-sabotaging behaviours.

And where do most of these beliefs and phrases come from?

Our parents!

And they probably inherited their beliefs from their parents and so on. You can choose to either carry on the generational pattern and continue to struggle financially with all the ensuing self-belief and confidence issues. Or you can change it by changing the words and phrases you use to describe money.

So how do we start to work on this? Take a quiet moment and write down everything that comes to mind about money. Every phrase, every thought no matter how dark or negative. Write them down so you can see them clearly and recognise the impact they might be having on your life.

Once you have a list of negative or poor phrases and beliefs about money, take the time to work out the opposite statement for each thought. Then, whenever you hear yourself say the negative phrase, immediately repeat to yourself the positive opposite. The more you do this, the more you start to recode your unconscious brain to have a more positive mindset around money.

For example,

The negative phrase: Money doesn't grow on trees

Becomes: Money is abundant and I find it everywhere

Something to note – whilst the changes this simple exercise can create are profound; they are rarely quick. Changing patterns we've had since childhood takes time and consistent effort so please be patient with yourself and just keep putting in

the work. If you stick to it, you are guaranteed to transform your mindset and therefore your reality! However, too few people do it for long enough to see a result and give up discouraged resigning themselves to struggling financially for the rest of their lives.

But if you put in the work consistently, for a long enough duration, you'll start to notice that as your Money Mindset changes, you'll notice that your Financial Habits start improving automatically. If you choose to start implementing positive Financial Habits sooner, you'll speed up your progress even faster.

Financial Habits

There are as many positive Financial Habits as there are negative ones, so for simplicity sake, I'm going to list the top 3 Habits I suggest to everyone because these are the ones that made the biggest impact in my life.

1. Save 10% of whatever you make

If you don't save anything, you'll never change your financial reality. No savings means you'll have to go into debt to deal with any financial challenges or purchases you make over and above your monthly income.

Think of savings as the money you pay yourself in the future. By putting it aside now, you are making sure your future self has money when it needs it. If you have no savings, you have no safety net in case anything goes wrong.

The important thing with savings is that they actually happen! I know this might sound obvious, yet far too many of us go through the month paying everything and everyone else and find there's nothing left to pay ourselves in terms of saving. The only way to change this is to make a commitment to save the first 10% of whatever you earn and put it into a savings account that you do not touch. Avoid waiting until the end of the month because there won't be anything left. By paying yourself first, you ensure it happens and even if you're on a low income and can't conceive how to find an extra 10% money, you'll find, perhaps surprisingly, as the months go by you'll actually have enough money to save alongside all your other expenditure.

Watching your savings grow will build your sense of security. This leads to the justified belief that you'll be better able to cope with whatever life throws at you which in turns leads to increased confidence.

2. Get clarity on your finances

Get clear on what you have and what you don't. Far too many people have no idea of how much they have in monetary terms and also too little clarity on what they actually owe on that amount, such as mortgages, credit card debts, car loans etc.

Not knowing what you have means you don't know what level of security you have. For example, if everything went wrong and you suddenly needed a large amount of cash, such as to pay for an emergency operation, how much could you lay your hands on if you sold everything you have? Knowing this number lets you know how long you could survive for without income and if the worst case scenario happens. This is where confidence or fear comes from – knowing whether you could survive or not!

Add up the real value of everything you own. By real value I mean what you would get today if you sold it, not what you paid for it as this is probably a very different number!

Whatever this number is, now deduct from it the total amount of debt you have. For example, you house might be worth £100,000 if you sold it. Yet if the mortgage is £70,000 you personally only own £30,000.

For some of you, deducting what you owe from what you have will produce a positive figure – congratulations! The larger this number, the longer you could survive without income for and the greater your confidence will be.

Some of you will come up with a negative or minus figure. I understand how depressing this can feel, yet the great thing is that you are now connected with your real financial reality and how important it is to change it fast!

Recognising my own levels of debt and that I was facing financial ruin was the first step towards changing it forever. Writing this chapter, 7 years after that heart-breaking realisation, after consistent and sometimes back-breaking effort, I am now in the position where I never have to work again and my family is looked after financially by what I've created no matter what happens. Was it easy? Hell no! But it was definitely worth it and my mindset and confidence have improved exponentially!

3. Track your progress

Knowing what comes in and what goes out every month allows you know how quickly you are sinking or rising. Whilst this might sound dramatic, if you don't know what you make or spend each month, it leads to a lack of security and clarity. Most people operate on the basis that if there's money left in their account at the end of the month, then it's ok. Yet this doesn't give any insight as to where the rest of the money has gone and whether it's helped you increase or decrease your financial security.

First get clear on what you actually earn or make each month. If it fluctuates or varies every month, what is the average amount? Knowing this lets you know what you have to work with.

Now start tracking your expenses so you know what goes out each month. Write down everything you spend each day for an entire month. You can use pen and paper, or there are many free Apps that allow you to track expenses. Write down absolutely everything – no exceptions, no matter how small. This exercise is double edged as by writing down everything, you'll see where your money actually goes. And by having to write down and admit what you are spending your money on, it will automatically make you assess whether you want to spend that money or not, therefore helping you reduce any outgoings that are perhaps unnecessary.

Knowing what you have to play with each month and making conscious choices over what you spend your money on, will increase your financial security and massively boost your confidence.

Whilst some of the steps I've outlined above, might seem simplistic and easy to dismiss, recognise that any resistance to taking action could indicate an area you could massively benefit from working on. Improving your financial security by working on your Money Mindset and your Financial Habits is THE most effective way I know to create true and lasting confidence. Knowing you can survive financially and look after your loved ones no matter what life throws at you creates a level of self-belief and self-worth that most people unfortunately never experience. Put in the time and the effort to transform your financial reality and you'll develop unshakeable confidence.

Wishing you every success!

Chris

Chris Lambert-Gorwyn

Growing Heart Centred Businesses from Passion to Profit

www.chrisandkarene.com

chris@heartcentredbusiness.com

Phone: +44(0)333 987 4245

Chris is the bestselling author of Grow Your Heart Centred Business from Passion to Profit and considered the UK's #1 Business and Wealth Mentor. Living in London with his wife Karene and daughter Mya, Chris and Karene support Practitioners and Experts to build heart centred businesses where they make a bigger difference in the world and get paid what they're truly worth. Chris and Karene's clients typically increase their income by £50,000-£100,000 within 12 months of implementing their systems.

A Final Thought From The Author

11 Habits Of Mentally Strong People

The bedrock of confidence is mental strength. Mental strength, also known as resilience or fortitude is one of the key determinants of success in any endeavour. This is what creates true confidence.

We all reach critical points in our lives where our mental strength is tested. It might be a difficult friend or colleague, a dead-end job, or a struggling relationship. Whatever the challenge, you have to be strong, see things through a new lens, and take decisive action if you want to move through it successfully. The more often we do this, the easier it becomes and the more our confidence grows.

It sounds easy. We all want good friends, good jobs, and good relationships.

But it isn't.

It's challenging to be mentally strong, especially when you feel stuck. The ability to break the mold and take a bold new direction requires that extra grit, daring, and spunk that only the mentally strongest people have.

It's fascinating how mentally strong people set themselves apart from the crowd. Where others see impenetrable barriers, they see challenges to overcome.

When Thomas Edison's factory burned to the ground in 1914, destroying one-of-a-kind prototypes and causing $23 million in damage, Edison's response was simple:

"Thank goodness all our mistakes were burned up. Now we can start fresh again."

Edison's reaction is the epitome of mental strength—seeing opportunity and taking action when things look bleak.

There are habits you can develop to improve your mental strength. In fact, the hallmarks of mentally strong people are actually strategies that you can begin using today to build your own resilience, confidence and levels of success.

The 11 Top Habits of Mentally Strong people are:

Mentally strong people are emotionally intelligent.

Emotional intelligence is the cornerstone of mental strength. You cannot be mentally strong without the ability to fully understand and tolerate strong negative emotions and do something productive with them. Moments that test your mental strength are ultimately testing your emotional intelligence (EQ).

Unlike your IQ, which is fixed, your EQ is a flexible skill that you can improve with understanding and effort. It's no wonder that 90% of top performers have high EQs and people with high EQs earn $28,000 more annually (on average) than their lower-EQ counterparts. Unfortunately, EQ skills are in short supply. TalentSmart has tested more than a million people and found that just 36% of these people are able to accurately identify their emotions as they happen.

They're confident.

Mentally strong people subscribe to Ford's notion that your mentality has a powerful effect on your ability to succeed. This notion isn't just a motivational tool—it's a fact. A recent study at the University of Melbourne showed that confident people went on to earn higher wages and get promoted more quickly than others did.

True confidence—as opposed to the false confidence people project to mask their insecurities—has a look all its own. Mentally strong people have an upper hand over the doubtful and the skittish because their confidence inspires others and helps them to make things happen.

They say no.

Research conducted at UC Berkeley showed that the more difficulty you have saying no, the more likely you are to experience stress, burnout, and even depression. Mentally strong people know that saying no is healthy, and they have the self-esteem and foresight to make their „Nos" clear.

When it's time to say no, mentally strong people avoid phrases such as "I don't think I can" or "I'm not certain." They say no with confidence because they know that saying no to a new commitment honors their existing commitments and gives them the opportunity to successfully fulfill them.

The mentally strong also know how to exert self-control by saying no to themselves. They delay gratification and avoid impulsive action that causes harm.

They neutralize difficult people.

Dealing with difficult people is frustrating and

exhausting for most. Mentally strong people control their interactions with toxic people by keeping their feelings in check. When they need to confront a toxic person, they approach the situation rationally. They identify their emotions and don't allow anger or frustration to fuel the chaos. They also consider the difficult person's standpoint and are able to find common ground and solutions to problems. Even when things completely derail, mentally strong people are able to take the toxic person with a ‚grain of salt' to avoid letting him or her bring them down.

They embrace change.

Mentally strong people are flexible and are constantly adapting. They know that fear of change is paralyzing and a major threat to their success and happiness. They look for change that is lurking just around the corner, and they form a plan of action should these changes occur.

Only when you embrace change can you find the good in it. You need to have an open mind and open arms if you're going to recognize, and capitalise on, the opportunities that change creates.

They embrace failure.

Mentally strong people embrace failure because they know that the road to success is paved with it. No one ever experienced true success without first embracing failure. By revealing when you're on the wrong path, your mistakes pave the way for you to succeed. The biggest breakthroughs typically come when you're feeling the most frustrated and the most stuck. It's this frustration that forces you to think differently, to look outside the box, and to see the solution that you've been missing.

Yet, they don't dwell on mistakes.

Mentally strong people know that where you focus your attention determines your emotional state. When you fixate on the problems that you're facing, you create and prolong negative emotions and stress, which hinders performance. When you focus on actions to better yourself and your circumstances, you create a sense of personal efficacy, which produces positive emotions and improves performance. Mentally strong people distance themselves from their mistakes, but they do so without forgetting them. By keeping their mistakes at a safe distance, yet still handy enough to refer to, they are able to adapt and adjust for future success.

They don't compare themselves to others.

Mentally strong people don't pass judgment on other people because they know that everyone has something to offer, and they don't need to take other people down a notch in order to feel good about themselves. Comparing yourself to other people is limiting. Jealousy and resentment suck the life right out of you; they're massive energy-stealers. Mentally strong people don't waste time or energy sizing people up and worrying about whether or not they measure up. Instead of wasting your energy on jealousy, funnel that energy into appreciation. When you celebrate the success of other people, you both benefit.

They exercise.

A study conducted at the Eastern Ontario Research Institute found that people who exercised twice a week for 10 weeks felt more socially, intellectually, and athletically competent. They also rated their body image and self-esteem higher. Best of all, rather than the physical changes in their bodies being responsible for the uptick in confidence, which is key to mental strength, it was the immediate endorphin-fueled positivity from exercise that made all the difference.

They get enough sleep.

It's difficult to overstate the importance of sleep to increasing your mental strength. When you sleep, your brain removes toxic proteins, which are by-products of neural activity when you're awake. Unfortunately, your brain can remove them adequately only while you're asleep, so when you don't get enough sleep, the toxic proteins remain in your brain cells, wreaking havoc by impairing your ability to think—something no amount of caffeine can fix.

Mentally tough people know that their self-control, focus, and memory are all reduced when they don't get enough—or the right kind—of sleep, so they make quality sleep a top priority.

They're relentlessly positive.

Keep your eyes on the news for any length of time, and you'll see that it's just one endless cycle of war, violent attacks, fragile economies, failing companies, and environmental disasters. It's easy to think the world is headed downhill fast. And who knows? Maybe it is. But mentally strong people don't worry about that because they don't get caught up in things they can't control. Instead of trying to start a revolution overnight, they focus their energy on directing the two things that are completely within their power—their attention and their effort.

Try using any of these 11 habits in your life and see what impact it has on your mental health and therefore your confidence. If you're in doubt of whether you could successfully implement these habits or use them to create success, consider the words of Henry Ford...

"Whether you think you can or think you can't...

you're right." – Henry Ford

David Gil Cristobal

Website: www.davidgilcristobal.com

Email: david@davidgilcristobal.com

Phone: +41(0)79 311 04 61

David is a multi-bestselling author and considered Switzerland's leading Success and Wealth Mentor. Living in Basel with his wife Lea, David has spent more than 20 years helping others reach their highest levels of success. His products, events, coaching programs, and mentorship is designed to help you achieve more than you ever thought possible in less time.

Congratulations!

Now you've reached the end of the book, the action starts. Depending on how you have read this book, now might be the time to go back and take some notes or even re-read a couple of chapters.

What are your key learnings from what you've read?

What are the top 5 things that you can perhaps change, tweak or add into your life to make a difference based on what you have read? Take the time to write these down as the act of writing will help cement them in your mind.

1.

2.

3.

4.

5.

Reading is of course valuable, yet it's taking action on what we've learned that creates change in our lives. Change can be both scary and exciting because it means doing things differently and creating a different and perhaps unknown outcome. With what you've learned from this book and the actions you're now going to take, what might now be possible for you, your family or loved ones?

Often, we look at the negatives of change and keep ourselves stuck because it feels safer. We would challenge you to look at the positives of change and get yourself moving physically or metaphorically. List out 5 great things that might be possible for you if you started adopting some of the suggestions from this book:

1.

2.

3.

4.

5.

By the way, if you found it challenging fill in this list, perhaps going back and re-reading or studying some of the chapters could help you get clear on what could become possible for you now.

However, if you're struggling with the idea of re-reading a book or 'studying' it then perhaps this example might help. As a Bikram yoga devotee, Karene used to do the same 26 postures in every Bikram yoga class and she used to do 1 or 2 classes every day. Yet every time, each class was different because she was different. Perhaps she had slept differently, or had different experiences meaning she had more or less energy to bring to class. Some days her favourite posture turned out to be the one she struggled with the most; or the one posture she didn't usually like became the one that made a real difference to her mood that day! It is same with books....there is always something new to 'see' when we re-read something because each time we read it, we are different. We have a different mindset and different emotions because we've had different experiences since we last read the book. This means we are going to notice and remember different things when we re-read it.

So, by all means if you have enjoyed this book, pass it on to a friend, colleague or loved one and also revisit and re-read it for the lessons, stories and possibilities it might provide for you in the future. We know that not all of the authors, stories or experiences will resonate with you first time round and yet others may be the start of a new journey for you. We encourage you to reach out personally to those authors who ‘spoke’ to you to see what else they might be able to offer as support on your journey or just to feed back the difference their words have made for you.

We all go through life as individuals, however, it is the experience of relating to other humans where the magic happens. When we relate to others, we learn more about ourselves. We hope that this book has allowed you to ‘meet’ some more people and gain a deeper understanding of yourself.

We, and the authors who have made this possible, wish you every success with your journey.

Best wishes

Chris, Karene & David

About The Authors & HCB Publishing

David Gil Cristobal turns people into brands so they earn what they are worth and conquer the box seat in their customer's head. With more than three decades experience in the sports and business arena, David had a long career as a professional soccer player, before co-founding Eerion Performance, one of Switzerland's top health and fitness organisations, and launching Fitness Fortune University where he turns health and fitness professionals into elite fitness businesses in as little as 90 days. His clients typically increase their income by $50,000-100,000 within 12 months of implementing his systems. He has personally trained more than 1000 company teams in how to scale their businesses to new levels and experts in how to build 6 figure businesses.

Armed with a masters degree in business management and leadership, having built multiple 5, 6, and 7 figure businesses of his own, spoken to more than 100,000 people at Business and Financial conferences around the world in 13 different countries on 3 different continents, meeting business authorities and opinion leaders such as Sir Richard Branson, Tony Robbins, Kevin Harrington, Kane & Alessia Minkus and Herman Scherer, best-selling author off 5 books in 2 different languages, David speaks 6 languages, and has starred in a motion picture.

Chris and Karene Lambert-Gorwyn are the founders of Heart Centred Business Ltd and the authors of the #1 Amazon Best-Selling Book, Grow Your Heart Centred

Business from Passion to Profit. Having built multiple 5, 6 and 7 figure businesses of their own, Chris & Karene have been humbled with numerous Business Awards. They've spoken at Business and Financial conferences around the world in 14 different countries on 4 different continents, meeting business titans such as Sir Richard Branson, Les Brown, Tony Robbins, Randi Zuckerberg, Kevin Harrington, Gill Fielding, Nick James, Kane & Alessia Minkus and Robert & Kim Kiyosaki.

Chris & Karene grow Heart Centred Businesses and their clients typically increase their income by £50,000-100,000 within 12 months of implementing their systems. Teaching the right things in the right order, Chris & Karene have personally trained more than 3000 practitioners and experts how to build 6 figure businesses.

HCB Publishing

Chris, Karene and David founded HCB Publishing to help more business owners share their expertise with the world

Do you have a special skill or expertise? Would you be curious to know how to use books to exponentially grow your business?

If you want to talk further and get direct support from Chris, Karene and David to take your business and income to a totally different level, register on the link below and explore how you might be able to achieve your dreams much quicker than you thought by working together.

As successful business owners, we've coached and trained thousands of clients to success. We're fortunate to make our living doing what we love, which is helping other experts to become successful.

But, it wasn't always easy. We all started out like most authors with no platform, no database, no experience, and a whole lot of questions. We spent many years figuring out how to sell books from scratch, build businesses, learn what works, and what doesn't. But you don't have to learn the hard way like we did. We're here to share with you what works and what doesn't so you can write and sell your expertise via books and increase your reputation and your income.

Take the next step in your Author Career and work with us directly. Click on the link below for more details about your next steps:

www.hcbpublishing.com

Work with us and learn how to use books to grow your income and your business!

Printed in Great Britain
by Amazon

57742373R00093